The Lion Cub of Prague

The Lion Cub of Prague

Thought, Kabbala, Hashkafa
from Gur Arye

A commentary on Rashi on the Torah by
Morenu Harav Yehuda Loewe ben Betzalel

THE MAHARAL OF PRAGUE

❧ GENESIS ❧

Moshe David Kuhr, MD, MPH, FAAP

gefen גפן
publishing house בית הוצאה לאור גפן
JERUSALEM • NEW YORK Est. 1981

Cover design: Benjie Herskowitz, Etc. Studios
Typesetting: Raphaël Freeman, Renana Typesetting

ISBN: 978-965-229-825-6

1 3 5 7 9 8 6 4 2

Gefen Publishing House Ltd.
6 Hatzvi Street
Jerusalem 94386, Israel
972-2-538-0247
orders@gefenpublishing.com

Gefen Books
11 Edison Place
Springfield, NJ 07081
516-593-1234
orders@gefenpublishing.com

www.gefenpublishing.com

Printed in Israel   *Send for our free catalog*

Library of Congress Control Number: 2015931317

Abraham J. Twerski, M.D.
Gateway Rehabilitation Center
Aliquippa, PA 15001

(412) 766-8700

With publication of *The Lion Cub of Prague*, my dear friend, Dr. Moshe (Murray) Kuhr has made a significant contribution to students of Torah.

Dr. Kuhr is a dedicated Torah scholar, having attended the Talmudical Academy yeshivah in Baltimore. He continued his Torah study with a number of Torah scholars and various study partners. This prepared him admirably for *The Lion Cub of Prague*.

Dr. Kuhr labored diligently for ten years to unravel the works of the great Torah giant, Rabbi Yehudah Loewe, known as Maharal of Prague; one of the greatest sages of all time. Maharal was a prodigious writer, yet it is often difficult to tease out the meanings. Once these are elucidated, Maharal's profound wisdom and Torah insights become evident.

The Lion Cub of Prague is a selection of Maharal's comments on Rashi's Torah commentary. Dr. Kuhr has translated these and clarified their content, drawing upon other Maharal writings, with extensive sourcing and footnotes. Torah insights previously unavailable, especially to the English reader, are now available to us in a reader-friendly format. The selections on the parsha, which are of a unique nature, are nuclei for divrei Torah at the Shabbos table.

Hopefully, the appreciation of Maharal's great wisdom will stimulate Torah students to study his works, which are voluminous. Dr. Kuhr has titillated our curiosity, and we may look forward to his continuing to enlighten us with exposition of Maharal's works.

הרב דוב בערל וויין

שדרות בן מימון 15
ירושלים, עיה"ק

טל: 0515‑561 (02)
פקס: 1956‑567 (02)

16 Adar II 5768
23 March 2008

For many centuries, the writings of the Maharal of Prague have
been a source of wonder, education, knowledge and holiness for
the Jewish people. His seminal commentary to the Torah and
Rashi, Gur Aryeh, has been a classic since its first publication.
However, the wisdom and inspiration of the work has been hidden from much of the English-reading public till now. My friend,
Dr. Murray Kuhr, has painstakingly translated and elucidated this
work with grace, finesse and reverence. All those who value true
Torah scholarship will find Dr. Kuhr's work a treasure of Jewish
wisdom and tradition, philosophy and worldview.

May Dr. Kuhr be blessed to continue his noble work of scholarship for the benefit of all of Israel.

With Torah greetings,

Rabbi Berel Wein

Contents

The Lion Cub of Prague

Preface

For our tenth wedding anniversary, my dear wife, Phyllis, presented me with a set of *Mikraot Gedolot*, containing commentaries on *Tanach* [Bible]. This was an incentive to apply myself to the correction of a major failure of my yeshiva education, my inability to access Torah and commentaries on my own. With the help of Silverman's translation of the eleventh century commentary of Rabbenu Shlomo Yitzchaki, known to all by the acronym, Rashi, and Chavel's newly published translation of the thirteenth century commentary of Rabbenu Moshe ben Nachman [Ramban], I set out to master Torah on *Shabbat* afternoon along with my *chavruta* [learning partner], Len Ruder, who was just becoming a *chozer biteshuva* [newly observant], though he may not have known it at the time. We took our time, looked up most of the references in Chavel's notes, and inched our way through *Parashat Bereshit* over the course of a few years. Six years later, we moved from our home in the heartland, Dayton, Ohio; Len and family to Israel, and we to Monsey. The *chavruta* was reconstituted with illustrious Monsey additions and is now in its thirty-sixth year. Every *Shabbat* we gather to learn a few verses of Torah along with our intellectual forebears Onkelos, Rashi, Ramban, Torah Temima, and assorted others when there is a problem in interpretation. We are about to complete *Sefer Devarim* [Deuteronomy] thirty-six years later with the help of Hashem.

For our thirty-seventh wedding anniversary, my wife presented me with a set of *Meorot Gedolim* containing eleven supercommentaries on Rashi. Ready for a new challenge, I suggested to my dear friend, the noted *talmid chacham* [scholar] and surgeon, Yehuda Eliezri, that we learn Rashi again, with a supercommentary neither of us had studied. He suggested Gur Arye and I said, "Who is that?" He told me it was the Maharal of Prague. You see, the editor of *Mikraot Gedolot* had not seen fit to include the commentary, and none of my excellent teachers had ever directed me to it.

Gur Arye, which means lion cub, turned out to be a gold mine. Maharal, short for *Morenu Harav* [our master, the teacher] Loewe, a 16th century master teacher and original thinker, brought his formidable intellectual powers and immense fund of knowledge to interpret and defend the terse notes of his ancestor, Rashi, in an elaborate running commentary on all of the Five Books of Moses.

Rashi's 11th Century commentary attempts to present the Written Torah through the eyes of the rabbis and the prism of the Oral Torah and his notes are usually verbatim quotes of the words of the midrash and Talmud. However, he also explores the meaning of passages through etymology and grammatical anomalies. He often presents a quick "fix," enabling the student to get past a difficult passage or delve deeper if he wishes. It has often been said that he gently takes learners of Torah of all ages and stages by the hand.

The passage of four centuries and the advent of the printing press gave ample opportunity for the critics of Rashi's commentary to speak their piece. Ramban generally quotes Rashi and often disagrees on intellectual grounds, not feeling compelled to accept the version espoused by *Chazal* [the rabbis of blessed memory]. Re'em, Rav Eliahu Mizrachi [15th century Constantinople], asks questions on Rashi, which Maharal usually cites and addresses, but with the intent to offer an alternate answer. Others too have asked on and attacked Rashi through the years. Maharal's particular purpose has been to come to Rashi's defense and to the defense of the interpretations of *Chazal* upon whom Rashi's commentary is based.

We soon discovered the recently published *Gur Arye*

Hashalem with the excellent notes of Rabbi Yehoshua David Hartman of Jerusalem. Rabbi Hartman has referenced and indexed the Gur Arye and other works of Maharal, as well as explaining any difficult passages. Most importantly, he cites important passages from other works by Maharal, bringing them to bear on the subject matter at hand. He is a major mentor of this project and has generously encouraged me to avail myself of his notes.

A few months into the study of the Gur Arye, I was so excited by it, I decided to translate it into English, and proceeded to do so longhand on legal pads. I ended up translating the first four *sidrot* [weekly portions] of *Sefer Bereshit* [Genesis]. I spoke of it with everyone I knew, and came to understand that no one would be interested in a translation. Translations are stilted and the nuances of the Hebrew are impossible to convey. Only Talmud sells well in translation, for some very special reasons. Maharal has a unique vocabulary that conveys his philosophy. Much of the Gur Arye is technical and arcane and of interest only to serious students of Rashi, and I wanted to open it up to the casual English reader. I wanted people to get as excited about it as I was.

This work, then, consists of selections of Maharal's thought. I have culled out less than one tenth of the Gur Arye on *Sefer Bereshit*, trying to preserve the master's literary style when possible. The selections are based on ethical content, uniqueness of thought, fundamental theological concepts, Kabbalistic nuance, and the wonders that I found in the text.

I owe my deepest debt of appreciation to the Holy One, blessed be He, Who has kept me alive, and sustained me, and brought me to this day. I pray that He will allow me the years to finish this project that I have just begun. I thank my wife for her encouragement and selfless devotion to me and my Gur Arye project, and my son, Menachem, my first editor, who taught me much about writing. At the outset of this project, my basic writing experience consisted of thirty-five years of prescriptions. I thank my *chavruta*, Yehuda Eliezri, who has taught me so much;

my *chavruta* by proxy, Rabbi Yehoshua David Hartman; and, my *Rabbi muvhak*, Rabbi Berel Wein.

Much gratitude to Yaacov Peterseil and Daniella Barak at Devora Publishing Company, and to my editor, Abe Weshler, who were all a delight to work with.

I thank my teachers, Rashi, Ramban, and Maharal, and look forward to sitting at their feet in the World to Come.

CRITERIA FOR SELECTION

Yesodei Emuna [foundations of Jewish faith]. When Maharal elaborates on basic principles of our belief, he reveals to us his unique outlook or states the principles in such a way as to enhance our understanding. Theological content tends to lead to selection in the sense that what interests me is likely to interest the reader.

Mussar [ethics; literally, admonition]. One of my most influential teachers, Rabbi Harry Rottenberg, of blessed memory, once told me that the key to the Gur Arye is its *mussar* content. Any selection that has a message that tells us how to lead a better life is included in this work.

Parshanut [mechanics of interpretation]. I have learned through the Gur Arye how the authors of the midrash take inconsistencies in tense, gender, extra or missing letters, dots in the Masoretic text, etc., and transform them into new narrative or messages. Maharal is keen on elaborating how it is that the midrash quoted by Rashi came to be. Some Gur Arye selections present "rules" that govern interpretation, such as how to deal with the multiple meanings that characterize words in the holy tongue.

Battles of the Titans. Those verses that generate disputes between the major commentators give us insight into the range of acceptable opinion. When *halacha* [law] is involved, a decision must be formulated in order to guide us with consistency and truth. *Sefer Bereshit* is virtually all *agada* [legend], and is open to interpretation, and these disputes require no resolution. When the giants clash, it makes for good copy.

Kabbala. Jewish mystical thought abounded during Maharal's

time. Jewish thought was inalterably influenced by the appearance and popularization of Kabbala in the thirteenth Century. Previously an arcane, esoteric pursuit of the few, the revelation, or introduction, of the *Zohar* by Rabbi Moshe de Leon in Spain revolutionized Jewish thought. Ramban's major pursuit of Kabbala in his Gerona academy was, for the most part, not articulated in his commentary, except for notes virtually undecipherable to the ordinary student of his work, often followed by the cryptic comment, *hamayvin yavin* [the one who understands will understand]. Maharal, on the other hand, integrates Kabbala into his work seamlessly, often quoting from the *Sefer Yetzira*, the *Bahir*, and the *Zohar*, all classic works of Jewish mysticism. He also cites remarks from *Chazal* that he calls *nistar* [hidden], an early term for material of mystical content. Kabbalistic content is a criterion for inclusion.

Metaphysics and philosophy. Metaphysics is defined as the systematic study of the principles of being and knowledge, the doctrine of the essential nature of all that is real. Before the scientific revolution heralded by Newton a century after Maharal, metaphysics is how thinkers thought. The doctrinal nature of Maharal's thought should not dissuade the reader, but some of the more obtuse passages were not selected. Maharal reserves the designation "philosopher" to apply to Aristotle and his ilk, including Rambam. Our treatment of the Gur Arye is not intended to present a systematic understanding of Maharal's thought, but rather a deeper understanding of Rashi and the Torah by way of Maharal's unique insight.

A WORD ABOUT TRANSLATION

Acknowledging a debt of gratitude to those who toiled to make available to the English-speaking public the Hebrew texts of the Bible and its commentaries, I have come to the realization that no translation is satisfactory. The convention is that one word in Hebrew must be conveyed into one word in English, which promotes flow of the text and readability at the expense of meaning and truth. The translator must decide which of many meanings to convey, thus denying the reader alternate, but just as true, meanings.

A translation of Onkelos' Aramaic rendering of the Torah reads far differently than the Artscroll Stone edition translation or a translation based on Rashi. Rabbi Aryeh Kaplan's *The Living Torah* tries to address this by selecting one translation, then citing alternates in his notes at the bottom of the page. But he is still making the choice of alternatives for the reader. The reader should make his own choices. He should *learn* the text rather than *read* the text. I propose rendering the Hebrew word in transliteration in italics, followed by the various possible translations in parentheses.

THE BODY OF MAHARAL'S WORK

This book attempts to integrate other of Maharal's thought, with the Gur Arye. A brief summary of his work is in order. Five books correspond to the verse in *Divre Hayamim* [Chron. 1 29:11]:

Gedula, on the *Shabbat*, was lost.

Gevurot Hashem is on *Pesach*, the departure from Egypt, and miracles.

Tiferet Yisrael is on *Shavuot* and the giving of the Torah.

Netzach Yisrael is on *Tisha B'Av*, exile, and redemption.

Hod, on *Succot*, was lost.

Or Chadash is on *Purim*.

Ner Tamid is on *Chanuka* and world history.

Be'er Hagola deals with problems and inconsistencies in the works of our sages.

Netivot Olam are ethical works on subjects like truth, fear of heaven, modesty, etc.

Derech Hachaim is a commentary on Ethics of the Fathers.

Chidushei Agadot are comments on agadic selections of Talmud, recently recovered from the Oxford Library by Rabbi Aryeh Carmel, of blessed memory.

The page citations to the above-mentioned books used in the notes of this volume refer to the fifteen-volume set of the writings of Maharal in Hebrew, published in Bnai Brak, Israel, 1980. The **Gur Arye** citations are from Rabbi Yehoshua David Hartman's **Gur Arye Hashalem**, Machon Yerushalayim, 1991.

A Note to the Reader

The first two chapters of *Sefer Bereshit* are the most ethereal and difficult to comprehend. They, along with the Chariot chapter in *Yechezkel*, comprise the foundation texts for Kabbala.

Book 1: Maharal on Creation

Bereshit

STRIVE TO NOT NEED HASHEM'S MERCY

1:1. In the beginning, *Elokim* created heaven and earth.

Rashi: It does not say "Hashem created heaven and earth," for first it rose in His thoughts to create the world with Midat Hadin [*the Attribute of Strict Judgment*]. *But He saw the world could not endure, so He gave precedence to* Midat Harachamim [*the Attribute of Mercy*] *and joined it to* Midat Hadin. *Therefore it is written, "On the day of* Hashem Elokim's *making of earth and heaven"* [2:4].

Gur Arye: Why do we need to know Hashem's thoughts in creating the world? Why should we be concerned that He first thought to create it in Judgment? The answer is that the Torah comes to teach us an essential moral lesson: it would be better for a man to exist according to *Midat Hadin* and not come to require *Midat Harachamim*, for that was Hashem's first intent, His will and desire. Only because the world could not endure did He create it with *Midat Harachamim*. Fortunate is he who is able to endure Judgment and not need Mercy. Indeed, this matter is the main secret of the order of the world – that even though Hashem created the world with the Attribute of Judgment, its ongoing existence requires the Attribute of Mercy.[1] In the words of the midrash, this is what the Holy One, blessed be He, said: If I create the world with *Midat Harachamim* it would result in sinning ways; with *Midat Hadin* it could not endure. So I will create it with both and let it be that it endure.[2]

How do we know that *Elokim* is Judgment and *Hashem* is Mercy? *Elokim* is *Midat Hadin*,[3] which adds up in gematria to "He is Judge," but the name *Hashem* is *Midat HaRachamim*. In *AT-BaSh* [transposed alphabet] the name of *Hashem* is *MTzPTz*[4] and its numerical equivalent is *berachamim* [in mercy].[5] Additionally, the four letter name, *Hashem*, refers to the Essence, the complete Good that provides for His creatures.[6]

MDK [Author's note]: The midrash exploits the variation of God's name in the first two chapters that describe creation. Gur Arye formulates the moral lesson in Rashi's midrash, that Hashem is telling us He would prefer for His creations to just do His will and not need His mercy when they fail to do it.

Gematria is the sum of the numerical equivalence of the Hebrew letters. The first ten letters of the Hebrew alphabet have the numerical value of 1–10. The second nine letters are multiples of ten, 20–100. The last three are multiples of 100, 200–400. In ATBaSh, the

---

1. Chidushei Agadot on B.M. 88a, 3:52: The lower spheres are material and physical, and materiality cannot stand up to Judgment, for Judgment is spiritual. Materiality can only endure from the aspect of Mercy. See Netiv Gemilut Chesed 5, 1:164b.
2. BR 12:15.
3. BR 33:3
4. Zohar 2:262
5. See Gur Arye 18:23[48] and 30:6[8]
6. Rashi, Deut. 3:24: "Your Greatness – this is the attribute of Your goodness"; also Rashi, Num. 17:14 and Maharal, Netivot Ha'avoda 18, 1:138a: "On account of His great name – that sustenance is the endurance of man, and the four letter name implies sustenance and fulfillment to the world. Therefore David mentions [Ps. 136] "for His kindness endures forever" twenty-six times, after *Hashem* [whose *gematria* is 26]."

first letter, alef, *is transposed with the last letter,* tav; *the second,* bet, *with the second to last,* shin, *etc.*

I took the liberty of translating the Torah text differently from the Gur Arye's understanding of the word bereshit, *which I found most difficult to convey in English.*

SEPARATION OF THE LIGHT

> 1:4. Hashem saw the light was good and Hashem separated the light from the dark.

Rashi: We cannot understand this without the agada *[midrashic interpretation]. He saw that the light does not deserve that the wicked use it so He set it aside for the righteous in the future.*

Gur Arye: In the other instances in the account of creation, it is written "and God saw that it was good"[7] only after the completion of the creation. Here, Hashem creates the light, then sees it is good, and then separates it, implying what He saw resulted in His action of separation. How did seeing that the light was good result in the subsequent act of separation? The verse seems to beg for an explanation. This is why we must turn to the words of the midrash [Hag. 12a] that when He saw the light was good, He determined it was not appropriate for the wicked to use, so He separated it and put it away for the righteous in the future. The wording of the verse intentionally generates a question for which the midrash supplies the answer. The interpretation is intrinsic to the verse.

Why did He create something and then store it away? Is it not written, "for Hashem is not a man that He should lie, and not the son of man that He should change His mind" [Num. 23:19]?[8] This cannot be a change of mind – the verse is narrating the reason for the hiding of the primordial light, not a change in His creation.

Why, then, if the light was not for this world, was it created during the six days of creation? The answer is, everything, even

---

7. Gen. 1:10, 1:12, 1:18, and others. Rashi, Gen. 1:7: Something finished is considered in its fullness and goodness.
8. Ramban asks here the same question and, unable to answer it, discards Rashi's midrash. Instead, he defines *amira*, the saying, "Let there be light," as bringing it into existence, and *reia*, seeing it was good, as establishing its continued existence.

the World to Come, was created then and "there is nothing new under the sun" [Ecc. 1:9]. The Rabbis explained [BR 12:10] that even the World to Come was created during the six days of creation as it is written, "For with [the letters] *Yud* and *Heh* was the creating of [both] worlds" [Isa. 26:4].[9]

MDK: This selection makes a strong point in parshanut [*mechanics of interpretation*], *that when the narrative has no simple explanation* [peshat], *the derived explanation of the rabbis* [derash, *midrash*] *fills the void to arrive at the truth.*

---

9. Men. 29b: This world was created with the letter *heh* and the World to Come with the letter *yud*. See Rashi, Gen. 2:4.

THE GENESIS OF EVIL

1:11. Let the earth sprout…trees of fruit yielding fruit…

Rashi: That the flavor of the tree shall be like the flavor of the fruit. But the earth did not do so. Rather, the earth brought forth "trees yielding fruit" but the tree itself was not fruit. Therefore, when Adam was cursed for his sin, the earth, too, was taken into account for its sin and was cursed.

Gur Arye: It is not that the earth transgressed the command of Hashem, for it has no evil inclination,[10] but it has *shinui* [changing, error, departure from order].[11] It is considered to be a lower level creation, for "heaven is Hashem's heaven, and the earth He gave to the children of man" [Ps. 115:15]. King David teaches us there is a difference between heaven and earth – heaven is in the higher sphere and earth in the lower. On account of this defect it perpetually lacks *shelemut* [harmony, completion, perfection].[12] King Shlomo said, "There is no righteous man *on earth* who will do good and not sin" [Eccl. 7:20]. This means it is impossible for man to be completely righteous on account of the defective earth from which he was created. Therefore, when the holy decree went forth: "tree of fruit bearing fruit," the earth was unable to fulfill the will of its Creator because of its lack of *shelemut*.

---

10. Gur Arye, Gen. 8:21[23]: The evil inclination only operates to make one fulfill a lust for something he does not have, and this only applies to humans.
11. Maharal, Netiv Haletzanut 1, 2:217b: The world is a physical world which has *shinui*, and all *shinui* is evil. Be'er Hagola 4:64b: *Shinui* applies to the lower spheres and not to the upper spheres. Chidushei Agadot on Er. 30b, 4:143b: Sin is *shinui* to a person, and a person cannot easily depart from order, but if he sins he establishes *shinui*.
12. Maharal, Ner Mitzva 8a: It is impossible that a creation be found in *shelemut*, for the earth is a lower creation…as it was *tohu vavohu* [1:2], and this deficiency teaches us of the deficiency that clings to all creatures. See 1:21[52]<194>.

When Adam sinned [3:6], the sin derived from a defect in him, whose origin was the earth, for he was created from earth [2:7], which was defective, making him defective. Thus he did not fulfill the command of his Creator.[13]

How did the earth come to "sin"? The earth receives *hashpaʿa* [providence, abundance] from the upper spheres and is a receiver with respect to them like the fruit is a receiver with respect to the tree.[14] The lowly receiver earth could only impart its power and taste to another receiver, the fruit, but did not impart power and taste to the tree, which had the higher status of provider. Therefore it brought forth fruit with taste and not tree with taste. If the tree had taste the deficient receiver fruit would have no purpose. When Adam sinned and took the fruit from the tree of knowledge [3:6] it was because of the affinity and desirability of fruit to him. Defective receiver Adam, made of defective receiver earth,

---

13. Maharal, Netiv Haʿemet 3, 1:204b and 203b.

14. Maharal, Derasha Leshabbat Hagadol 201b on the midrash [BR 20:7]: There are four *teshukot* [yearnings].... a woman's *teshuka* is only for her husband and the rain's *teshuka* is only for the earth: "The receiver loves the provider [woman-husband] and vice versa, the provider loves the receiver [rain-earth]." Netiv Hayetzer 4, 2:131a: For the rain is a provider and has no role without a receiver, so it needs the earth. Taʿan. 6b: Rain is the husband of earth. Gevurot Hashem 70:320b: In all of creation there is equality between heaven and earth. Sometimes, earth precedes heaven [2:4] and sometimes heaven precedes earth [1:1] to tell us they are equal [BR 1:15]. For the heaven is the upper sphere and considered the beginning of all, and the earth the lower sphere and the *shelemut* of all creation. Do not be surprised that earth has such an exalted status, given the lowliness, coarse materiality, and ugliness in it. Earth did not earn this exalted status but it is the *shelemut* of creation. Gur Arye, Ex. 15:17: The same way the right and the left together make up the man, and there is no left without right nor right without left, heaven and earth make up the existence of the world and its *shelemut*. Only the earth is the left and not as important and the heaven the right and more important. See 28:17[23] and Netiv Hatorah 16, 1:70b and Netzach Yisrael 8:52b.

lusts for the receiver fruit, for like likes like – similar entities attract one another.[15]

By removing the fruit from the tree, the receiver from the provider, he made it the main entity. He was warned not to eat this particular fruit, which was located in the center of the garden, fitting to be the main tree.[16] Anything in the center is fitting to be the main entity,[17] and Adam is drawn to the receiver and makes it the main entity even though it is defective. The punishment comes to both earth and Adam for separating the fruit from the tree [3:17].

Later, Rashi explains his parable as to why the earth was cursed, that one curses the breasts of a mother that fed a criminal. When Adam created of earth sinned, Hashem cursed the earth. Adam's origin from earth caused him to sin, as earth is materiality, as it is written: "You are earth and to earth you shall return."[18] The mother who gave birth to the son is the reason for the sin of the son, for she gave the material out of which he was created.[19] Rashi explains there that on account of the earth's "transgression" here it was cursed at that point. There are two complimentary

---

15. Netiv Hayetzer 4, 2:131a: In midrash [BR 20:7] there are four *teshukot*…the *teshuka* of the evil inclination is only for Kayin and his friends, and the *teshuka* of the Holy One, blessed be He, is only for Israel…The evil inclination cleaves to the wicked because evil sticks to that which is prepared for it, the wicked…. for similar entities love and connect with each other…Therefore Hashem, who is the complete Good has *teshuka* for the good, that is Israel.

16. See Rashi 3:3 and 2:9[27].

17. Gur Arye 2:7[21]: Every thing that is in the center is in balance and does not incline to one of the extremes, and it is the choicest. Meg. 21b: The center is *shalem* [complete, perfect]. See Netzach Yisrael 59:215a, Tiferet Yisrael 70:217b, Ner Mitzva 8a, and Be'er Hagola 6:131a.

18. Gen. 3:19. Derech Hachaim to Ab. 4:11, 182b: Materiality causes sin, for without it man would be like an angel, without sin at all. Netiv Hateshuva 4, 2:157b: Sin comes from the material body, not the soul. However, Gur Arye 6:6[11] cites a dispute in BR 27:4. One opinion is that sin comes from the soul as well while the other opinion feels that sin comes only from the body.

19. Gur Arye 35:8[6]: The evil of Esav came from Rivka, not Yitzchak.

accounts in the midrash, one attributing the curse on the earth to the defective tree and the other to Adam's sin.

MDK: This beautiful parable is rendered in the style of the master with minimal alteration of the original text. The footnotes are worthwhile tangential excursions, but their incorporation into the heavily laden text would be awkward here. Maharal's metaphysical construct of mashpia/mekabel [*provider/receiver dichotomy*] *is introduced here.*

THE MEAL OF LEVIATHAN

1:21. And Hashem created the great sea-giants.

Rashi: These are large fish in the sea. In the words of the midrash this is the leviathan and his mate. He created them male and female, then killed the female and salted it away for the righteous in the future. If they were to reproduce and multiply the world would not endure in the face of them.

Gur Arye: Baba Batra [74b] quotes Psalms [104:26]: "You created the leviathan to frolic with" – it would be unseemly for Him to frolic with a female. This is strange to some, who do not know the paths of wisdom, and if they would, they would be amazed at the wisdom in the hearts of the rabbis and say, "Blessed is He who passed His wisdom to those who fear Him" [Ber. 58a]. I will reveal part of the understanding of this saying – perhaps the reader will get more of it on his own.

Rav Yehuda says in the name of Rav [B.B. 74b]: The Holy One, blessed be He, created everything in His world male and female, even the leviathan, but the union of the two together would be destructive for the world. What did Hashem do? He castrated the male and killed the female and salted it away for the righteous in the future. Understand that the *shelemut* [harmony, completion, perfection] is the pairing of male and female, called *zug* [pair, couple] because they couple with each other. Man is not called Adam unless he has his mate, as it is written, "Male and female He created them and called their name Adam" [5:2].[20] This story

---

20. Chidushei Agadot on B.B. 74b, 3:106a: Since the lower creations are not of the degree and loftiness of the upper creations, Hashem wanted to give merit to man and the other lower creatures, so He made them male and female from the perspective "Two are better than one" [Eccl. 4:9]. Each has what the other does not. "I will make a helper against him" [Gen. 2:18] applies to all the lower creatures. The coupling of male and female results in *shelemut* greater than any other aspect that applies to them. Not just that the woman helps him do

tells us there are creatures the world cannot accept on account of their extreme characteristics, so that had they coupled the world could not endure. Rashbam explains that this is simply because their offspring would be numerous. However, the main reason is their coupling, for they would destroy the world with their power when they would be together. The male alone does not have such power and the world could endure with him.

The statement, "He salted it away for the righteous in the future," from which it is understood that the righteous in the future eat, is disturbing to people, that in that holy place there should be eating and drinking, which implies a lack of *shelemut*. Moshe on the mountain "did not eat bread or drink water" [Ex. 34:28]. Likewise Eliahu.[21] Also Berachot 17a states, "The World to Come has no eating or drinking, but the righteous sit with their crowns on their heads and benefit from the radiance of the *Shechina* [Divine Presence]." To understand this you must walk perfectly in the words of the sages. Trustworthy witnesses attest these words cannot be interpreted simply. Kohelet Rabba [1:8] states: "All the prophets saw the Meal but no one saw its reward except Hashem Himself."[22] This reward is the World to Come, where there is no eating or drinking, only sitting with crowns. They will not need eating, meaning *kiyum* [fulfillment, continued existence], for this they will have received already at the Meal.[23] This Meal will

---

work or that they will have offspring – the act of coupling of the two is the *shelemut* of creation. The meaning of "even the leviathan was created male and female" is that even though the leviathan is not a physical creature, it was created male and female too. In the lower world single is abnormal and deficient. On sexual coupling, see Gevurot HaShem 56:249a, Be'er Hagola 2:36a and 35:17[12] where Maharal wrote: The female is the harmonious completion of the male.

21. Kings 1 19:8: And he went with the power of this meal forty days and forty nights to Hashem's mountain, Chorev.
22. 1:8. See Yalkut Shimoni, Isa. 50:8.
23. Er. 22a: Today to do them and tomorrow to receive reward. See Ramchal, Mesilat Yesharim, ch. 1. Derech Hachaim on 3:16, 152b repeats this: The meal of the leviathan will just precede the entry to the World to Come.

not be as our bodily eating, which arises from the power of desire, but rather a meal of satisfaction and *kiyum*. Eating in this world means the absorption of natural energy,[24] which does not apply in the World to Come. If natural man is fed physical food, spiritual man is fed *kiyum* and sustenance, which is spiritual food. Consider the nature of what is eaten – man eats refined food, meat and bread, while animals eat coarse grain, all of which are physical foods. If the Meal would be bread and wine or other physical foods, that would be very troublesome. But since the Meal is leviathan and the "cattle of one thousand mountains" [B.B. 74b], and "wine kept for the future" [Ber. 34b] and "*ziz*[25] of my field" [Ps. 50:11] – all these are spiritual and fitting for the Meal.[26]

Please note that Rabbi Akiva held that angels ate bread, from David's statement, "the bread of angels man ate" [Ps. 78:25]. Rabbi Yishmael said: "Tell Rabbi Akiva he errs, for did Moshe not say, 'I did not eat bread or drink water' [Deut. 9:9]?" Rabbi Akiva held that the angels eat this Meal, for all need sustenance from the *Ila* [Prime Cause, Maharal's expression for the Creator], for it is from His providence that all endure. Rabbi Yishmael held that the angels do not need sustenance, as they are not incomplete like man who needs food for *kiyum* [survival, fulfillment].[27] Understand this well.

Therefore man will have this Meal with which he will come to possess a high level never again to require food. When Moshe our teacher went on high to receive the Torah he entered the domain of the angels [Shab. 68b], hence he did not eat bread [Ex. 34:28]. Likewise, Eliahu [Kings I 19:8]. Now, how can you question the words of the sages? Eating pertained to Adam in the Garden of Eden as we learn from "You shall surely eat from all the trees

---

24. Ramban 2:17: Man's eating after he was penalized with mortality is replacement of a deficit in energy [Rabbi Chavel's rendering].
25. Rashi, Ps. 50:11: creeper. Gur Arye here: a bird.
26. Chidushei Agadot on B.B. 74b, 3:105a: Food refers to that which man incorporates into himself that will complete him, even if it is not physical.
27. Ramban, Ex. 16:6.

of the garden" [Gen. 2:16], and there is no question that Adam's level before the sin was very high.[28] Here also, one could say with respect to the Meal of the righteous, just as the spiritual Adam ate, why not the righteous?[29] They could eat the Meal, attain *kiyum*, then enter the World to Come.[30] Note Adam's eating from the tree of life would confer immortality [Gen. 3:22] as he would acquire his *kiyum*. The Meal abundantly provides spiritual nutrition from Hashem Himself.[31]

The leviathan and the cattle of a thousand mountains, just like the fruits of the Garden of Eden, are completely different and in no way connected to what we have now. The leviathan relates to water and the cattle to the earth.[32] The *ziz* of my field is in the atmosphere of heaven, so that nothing is lacking – earth, water, and air [heaven] include all of creation. There is a fourth special category – derived from fruit and made into drink later.[33] As in this world, the food in the future is acquisition and completion, incorporation and replenishment – the only difference is a change in spiritual level. Eating results in the kind of *shelemut* appropriate

---

28. Rashi, Deut. 4:32: The stature of Adam was from the earth to the heaven. From Sanh. 38b.

29. Continuation of footnote 20 on Deut. 7:16: "And you shall consume all the nations": Every nation has some substance or level, and Israel will assimilate that special substance and acquire *shelemut*.

30. Continuation of footnote 20: Do not say that the Meal is the level of the world to come. Eating it is replenishing the deficit and there is no deficit in the world to come, where *kiyum* is from Hashem himself, as they say the righteous "benefit from the radiance of the Divine Presence." See Netiv Hatorah 3, 1:13b and Derech Hachaim on Ab. 3:17, 152b: Man is only the result of Hashem, the *Ila* [Prime Cause], and cannot achieve *shelemut* on his own, but rather, the *Ila* perfects him.

31. See Num. R. 13:1.

32. Continuation of footnote 20: Water relates to the special characteristic of being provided by the right hand [Zohar 1:149b], and the cattle of a thousand mountains – which is the *shor habar* [wild ox] – are provided by the left [ibid. 248b]. When the righteous eat of these two they are perfected. See Gevurot Hashem 47:127b.

33. Ber. 34b: Wine guarded from the six days of creation.

to each world. Since man sees only the physical world it is difficult for him to grasp the concept of the World to Come.[34]

We noted at the outset that the leviathan was unfit for *shelemut* in this world, so the female was killed and salted for the righteous. Why create something to be killed? The answer is, many species were created and exist just for man's sustenance and *kiyum*. Why not do the opposite, kill and salt the male? Because being prepared to give one's self for others is a female characteristic,[35] a matter of her nature placed in her by Hashem, may He be blessed. These creatures lack mates, thus lack *shelemut*, and from this we know they are not of this world. May Hashem, may He be blessed, give us our portion among the living, that we may draw water from the wells of salvation [Isa. 12:3], and cause us to rejoice with those who look forward to His rejoicing, and may He spread over us the radiance of His Honor. Then we will rejoice with the four species of the meal.[36]

MDK: This selection is an example of rabbinic metaphysics, the logic of which is compelling. Like the previous selection, little alteration is made from the original text. Maharal uses the Meal to present a view of future events leading to the World to Come. A parallel account of the same subject appears in his discussion of the Gemara in Baba Batra, brought here in the footnotes.

---

34. Introduction to Gevurot Hashem 2: Why does the Torah not explicitly mention the World to Come? Because the Torah is the word of the Living God by the hand of the prophet and limited by the grasp of the prophet.

35. Continuation of footnote 20: The leviathan exists only in potential as it is prepared for a matter in the future – the righteous – and that is the purpose of its creation. This is more fitting for a female than a male.

36. This is a play on Lev. 23:40: "And you shall rejoice before Hashem your God seven days" referring to the four species taken on Succot [Rashi, Suk. 43b].

HANDMADE

1:27. And Hashem created man in his image.

Rashi: In the mold that was made for him.

Gur Arye: This means man's image rather than Hashem's image, for later in the verse, "He created him in Hashem's image," would be redundant.

Rashi: For everything was created through a statement of Hashem, but man was created by His hands.

Gur Arye: There needs to be a reason why man was handmade. The handiwork of the Holy One, blessed be He, is closer to Him than the spoken creations. One interpretation [unknown citation] is that the hands hinted at here refer to the heavens, considering the actions that Hashem does by the hand of the heavens,[37] of which there are ten, corresponding to the number of fingers. Through this celestial array Hashem created man to connect him to and establish him with the twelve constellations. The rabbis say [Shab. 53b]: "Man is different for he has *mazal* [astrologic influence, luck], and animals do not," as they were not created with this mold but rather by a saying. Consider a soul from the upper

---

37. Maharal, Netiv Hatorah 14, 1:60b, explaining Shab. 75a: "Anyone who knows how to reckon the seasons and the constellations and does not reckon them fails to appreciate Hashem's work." Regarding such a person, Isaiah 5:12 says, "the handiwork of Hashem they did not look at, and the creations of His hands they did not see." Says Maharal: "The seasons and the constellations which are in the heavens are the handiwork of Hashem, and the heavens are called the work of His hands, as it says in Psalms 8:4: 'For I will see your heavens, the work of your fingers.' Looking at the heavens, man can recognize the magnitude of the work He does and the enormity of His power and wisdom as he reckons their orbits and arrays. A person is obligated to know how to recognize his Creator."

spheres passing through the heavens on its journey to Earth to join the body of a fetus, influenced by the celestial bodies. Thus, they say that man has fixed in him twelve *mazalot* and seven moving bodies,[38] as is found in the astronomer's books.[39] But this explanation is incorrect, though this is not the proper place to refute it.

MDK: Maharal introduces an idea, leaves us no citation or reference to ground the idea in the holy works as he usually does, then quickly, cryptically, abandons it. He wants us to think about it, though.

---

38. Sun, Mercury, Venus, Moon, Saturn, Jupiter, Mars. See Or Chadash 101a.
39. Netiv Hatorah 14, 1:60b. Rabbi Pardes' notes, 744, discusses Maharal's relationship with the books of astronomy. Maharal knew Johannes Kepler, father of modern astronomy, from King Rudolph's court.

THE SANCTITY OF THE SEVEN

2:3. He abstained from all His work, which He created to do.

Rashi: He doubled the work that was fit to do on the Sabbath and did it on the sixth day.

Gur Arye: Why did He not do it on the seventh day, given that the sanctity of the seventh day is inherent? The Sabbath would be just as holy even if Hashem would continue to work on the seventh day. For the seventh is always the choicest[40] as it corresponds to *Aravot*, the seventh heaven, locus of the Holy and Sanctified Throne of Honor.[41] But He did no work on the seventh day, and the reason is most wondrous in the ordering of creation.[42] In the way the six days are fit for work, the seventh is inherently fit for rest. That is because the world is physical. Anything physical is bounded by six sides [North, East, South, West, up, down]. There

---

40. See Lev. R. 29:11.

41. Lev. R. 29:11: All sevens are always beloved, heavens…, lands: *Eretz, Adama, Arka, Ge, Tzia, Nesia, Tevel*, and it is written [Ps. 9:9]: "He will judge the world [*tevel*] in righteousness; He will judge the nations with uprightness." In generations: Adam, Shet, Enosh, Kenan, Mahalalel, Yered, Chanoch, and it is written [5:22]: "And Chanoch walked with Elokim." In patriarchs: Avraham, Yitzchak, Yaakov, Levi, Kehat, Amram, Moshe, and it is written [Ex. 19:3]: "And Moshe ascended to Elokim."…In years, the seventh is beloved as it says [Ex. 23:11]: "And in the seventh year you shall put it aside." In Sabbatical years, the seventh is beloved, as it says [Lev. 25:10]: "And you shall sanctify the fiftieth year." In days, as it says [2:3]: "And Hashem sanctified the seventh day." In months, as it is written [Lev. 23:24]: "And in the seventh month on the first of the month."

42. Tiferet Yisrael 40:122a. Also Derech Hachaim on 5:15, 255b: The number seven teaches about the level that connects the physical with the non-physical, and it is known that the number seven corresponds to six extremes and the center, which is called, "the Holy Place" [Sefer Hayashar, Ch. 4]. See also Chidushei Agadot on Sanh. 97a, 3:209a and Gevurot Hashem, 19:89a. Also see Chidushei Agadot on Ned. 39a, 214a and on R.H. 21b, 1:122a.

is another "boundary" separate unto itself – the center – an infinitely small dot occupying no space, which does not relate to anything physical, as the six sides do. Having no dimension, it relates to the non-physical – the spiritual. When Hashem created the six-sided world in six days, He rested on the seventh, corresponding to the center.

MDK: Abstinence from work, the hallmark of the Sabbath, is but a means to an end; the elevation and separation from the physical world to its infinitesimal, dimensionless, spiritual, central core, created as a consequence of Hashem's refraining from work on the seventh day.

THE SECRET OF THE HEH

2:4. These are the products of the heaven and the earth when they were created [*b'hiba'ream*].

Rashi: He created them with the letter heh, *as it says [Isa. 26:4]: In* Ya Hashem *is the Creator of worlds – with these two letters of the Name* [yud *and* heh], *He formed two worlds. The lesson is that this world was created with the* heh, *closed on all sides but open at the bottom hinting at the option of descending below to one's doom.*

Gur Arye: Rashi does not mention the opening near the top on the right.[43] If the wicked one who descended through the opening in the bottom should repent, the right hand of Hashem is extended to receive those who return[44] for whom He made an opening on the right.

MDK: The midrash explains an anomaly in the written Masoretic text. The heh *of* b'hiba'ream *is written smaller than the other letters, requiring the explanation of the midrash. B'hiba'ream can be rendered* b'heh bera'am [*with the letter* heh *He created them*], *explained so beautifully by Rashi and Gur Arye.*

---

43. See Maharal, Derasha Leshabbat Hagadol 79b. The upper part reaches out to us to pull us in through the opening on its right, our left.
44. Selichot prayers for the ten days of repentance: For Your right hand is outstretched to accept those who return. Zohar 1:23a: He gives His right hand, which is extended to receive those who return. Also see Pirke Derabbi Eliezer 43:3 and Netiv Hateshuva 8, 2:170b.

ADAM PRAYED AND THE RAIN FELL

> 2:5. *Hashem Elokim* had not caused rain to fall
> on the earth, and there was no man *la'avod* [to
> work, to serve] the earth.

Rashi: The reason for the lack of rain was the absence of man to work the earth and to recognize the goodness of the rain. When man came along, he knew that rain was necessary for the world to endure, so he prayed for it and it fell, and the trees and grasses sprouted.

Gur Arye: It is forbidden to do a favor for someone who does not appreciate it.[45] Therefore, as long as there was no human, He did not cause the rain to fall. Why then did He create everything else if no one would be there to appreciate its goodness? Why create, for example, the grasses? The answer is because the grasses were created for themselves – that is not called a favor. A favor is given to another, like the rain is given as a favor to the creatures that need it.

MDK: *The key to Rashi's midrash is the word* la'avod, *which means both to work and to serve, as in the priestly service. This is an example of the failure of a unitary translation to convey true meaning.*

---

45. Ber. 33a: If one lacks *dea* [understanding, consent], it is forbidden to have mercy on him. Sanh. 92a: Anyone who gives his bread to someone who lacks *dea* will have bad things happen to him. See Chidushei Agadot there, 3:163a: A favor needs someone to receive it or it will be rejected. Chidushei Agadot on Hul. 60b, 4:96a: The rain did not fall for there was, as yet, no connection between the upper and lower spheres. Man, who was of both spheres, intermediated between the two and brought the rain down from the heaven to the earth. See also Chidushei Agadot on Shab. 10a, 1:1 and Netiv Hatorah 8, 1:36b and Hul. 133a.

THE SECOND YUD

2:7. [*Vayyitzer*] And Hashem Elokim created the
man from dust of the earth.

Rashi: The two yuds in vayyitzer *connote two creations, this world
and the world of the resurrection of the dead.*

Gur Arye: Even though the second creation has not yet happened,
since man was created with the potential of that creation in the future, there are two creations in man now.[46] Therefore one creation
is explicit and the other indicated by the second *yud*, for it was
not complete and like a small dot.[47] However, the *Gemara* states
[Ber. 61a] that *vayyitzer* with two *yuds* relates to the midrash of the
two faces, as Rashi relates on "male and female He created them"
[1:25], that He first created them as one, with two faces, and later
split them.[48] Nevertheless, Rashi considered the words of Bereshit
Rabba [14:5] that the second *yud* explains both dualities of man's
creation, worlds and faces, and seized on the two worlds, because
we learn from this a matter of great importance – that man has a
portion in the World to Come.[49]

*MDK: Gur Arye reveals how Rashi edits the midrash, making the
selection that suits the point he wishes to make. The extra* yud *is*

---

46. Gur Arye 1:4[21]: All things – even that which will be in the future – were
created in the six days of Genesis, "and there is nothing new under the sun"
[Eccl. 1:9]. Tosafot, B.K. 16b quotes the midrash [BR 28:3]: There is a bone
in the spine of a person from which he will be created in the future. 10:8[2]:
Nimrod's idolatry was not mentioned explicitly since the service of Hashem
was not yet known. Also note Or Chadash 101a, Gevurot Hashem 17:80a, and
Rav Hutner's Pachad Yitzchak on Pesach, 52:3.
47. The smallness of the yud is discussed in Netiv Hatorah 1, 1:3, Derech Hachaim
3:153b, and Or Chadash 62b and 17:5[3].
48. Rashi comments on 1:25 on "male and female He created them," He first created them as one, with two faces, and later split them.
49. See Tiferet Yisrael 13:45a.

both a reference to the gender duality of the original man and the duality of man's existence in this world and the next. The latter carries the stronger mussar [ethical] *message, directing our eyes to the prize of the World to Come.*

THE NAVEL OF THE UNIVERSE

2:7. And Hashem *Elokim* created the man of dust from *the* earth.

Rashi: He collected his dust from the whole earth, from North, East, South, and West, so that wherever he dies the earth will absorb him.

Gur Arye: Animals are not created from the four corners of the earth, yet the earth absorbs them! To answer this, consider that the concept of burial only applies to people. Rabbi Yochanan said in the name of Rabbi Shimon bar Yochai [Sanh. 46b]: From where do we know that leaving a dead body unburied results in a transgression of a positive commandment? It is written [Deut. 21:23], "for you shall surely bury," and the *Gemara* learns from this that burial in earth is a commandment, as it is said [3:19], "for you are dust and to dust you will return." Elsewhere [BR 20:10], Rabbi Shimon bar Yochai said: From here is a hint of the resurrection of the dead from the Torah, as it does not say you are dust and to dust you will go, but it does say you will return. If he was not created from the entire earth, he could not return to the same earth, to be at one with it. This is a remarkable matter to those who understand the secret of man's burial. The matter of putting a body in the ground in burial is preparation for a future event.[50] Man has the potential to live in a future time and therefore is buried in the earth,[51] teaching us the potential for resurrection of the dead.

---

50. See Netiv Haosher 2, 2:227b.
51. Netiv Haosher 2, 2:229a: Earth is fit [to be used] for covering, and it is known that the dead need to be hidden; therefore, they are buried in the earth. Likewise, blood which needs to be covered…Three of the four elements [water, air, fire] are open, but earth is sealed and prepared for covering and sealing.

Something revealed is actual,[52] and something buried is potential.[53] The rabbis [Tanchuma, Pekudei 3] meant by "In every place the earth absorbs him" that the earth guards and protects him as it does a seed. He existed in potential in the earth before he was created, just as he does after he dies and is buried. Anything existing in potential requires something physical to bear it,[54] thus, the earth absorbs the body. Understand these matters well.

Rashi: Another interpretation is that He took the dust of that place about which it is said, "You shall make an altar of earth for Me" [Ex. 20:24]. Would that it be atonement for him that he should be able to endure.

Gur Arye: Rashi's second explanation of "dust of the earth," referring to the earth of the place of the Altar, seems to conflict with the four corners of the earth concept. This is resolved when one considers that the place of the Altar is the foundation of the entire world from which the world was drawn such that all earth was created from it. "Out of Zion, consummation of beauty" [Ps.

---

52. See Rashi and Gur Arye on Ex. 2:14 and Netzach Yisrael 15:61a and 24:22[26] and Chidushei Agadot on Sanh. 90a, "All Israel has a portion in the world to come," 3:176b.

53. Ket. 111b: The righteous will stand with their clothing, as one could logically deduce from a wheat kernel, which is buried naked and emerges with several layers of coverings. The righteous, who are buried in shrouds, will certainly emerge clothed. The analogy of the burial of the dead to the wheat kernel should be viewed in regard to the safekeeping of the object being placed in the ground for its future reemergence. See Tiferet Yisrael 10:31. Chidushei Agadot on Sot. 5b, 2:33b: "An arrogant person – his earth will not stir" means when he returns to his element [earth], this person will not stir the earth by sprouting and emerging in the resurrection of the dead like other people.

54. Derech Hachaim 2, 9:89b: Man, which Hashem created, has a body and bodily potential, and a soul and spiritual potential. The body is a carrier of the soul. Chidushei Agadot on Sanh. 96a, 201b: It is impossible for the soul not to have a bearer, for it cannot stand alone…See Or Chadash 148b and Netiv Hatorah 10, 1:45a and 14:13[21]<131> and 9:23[17]<68>.

50:2] is interpreted to mean [Tanchuma, Kedoshim 10] that the world was contained by and expanded from Zion – the place of the Altar. The center is considered equal to the whole, and the Altar is the center of the world.[55]

Rashi goes on to say that the earth of the place of the Altar would serve as atonement, which is problematic. The Altar does not atone without a sacrifice. To understand this, one must know the deep secrets of the Torah. The Altar is the center of the place of settlement of the earth, exactly between the extremes in each direction, in perfect balance and not inclining to any side, and it is the most choice.[56] The center is always the choicest – as the Land of Israel is the center of the settled world, it is chosen for sanctity, and since Yerushalayim is the center of the Land of Israel, it is more choice, and the Holy Temple is the most choice. One serves Hashem there because it is the center of settlement and not inclined to the extreme sides, which are less choice.[57] Creating man from the dirt of this place is in order that he can have atonement, and if sin should occur it would be easier to remove.[58] The inclination to one of the extremes causes sin,[59] and since man is created from the material of the center it is easier for him to return home to the center, and the sin will be removed from him. Consider the example of a pure, beautiful, smooth-skinned per-

---

55. Sanh. 37a: The Sanhedrin sits in the navel of the world. Rashi, Ex. 21:1. The place of the Sanhedrin is next to the place of the Altar.

56. Meg. 21b: The center is *shalem* [complete, perfect]. Tiferet Yisrael 22:68b: Centrality indicates choiceness. See ibid. 70:217b and Netzach Yisrael 59:215a and Be'er Hagola 6:131a and Gevurot Hashem, introduction 3:19.

57. Netzach Yisrael 55:252b: All who depart from the middle are ritually impure and evil. Derech Hachaim 2, 14:103b: You must know that death reaches a person when he turns aside from the center on which man was created and inclines to one of the sides...for death is an extreme, but balance and centrality is life.

58. See 1:11[33]<130>.

59. A person returns to his roots, as Rashi said of Hagar [21:21]: That is why people say that if you throw a stick straight up into the air it falls back to its point of origin, back to the place from which it was thrown.

son who gets soiled – it is easy for him to wash himself off. But if he was soiled and unseemly and rough to begin with,[60] the soiling invades him. The atonement of the place of the Altar serves to remove the poison. This is a very, very remarkable matter that deserves further study.

MDK: Here Rashi is faced with two fundamental principles of faith to help explain the earth from which man was made, and he chooses to present both. Each is cryptic, and the casual student of Rashi would likely glide past were it not for Gur Arye's insightful explication. The verse could otherwise be understood without the apparently redundant "from the earth" – where else does dirt come from? From these words we learn two of the important elements of our faith, burial/resurrection and centrality/Yerushalayim/atonement.

---

60. Gevurot Hashem 8:46a: Sin does not take hold of Israel because of sanctity. If a person whose essence is pure and beautiful becomes soiled with mud, washing off renders him pure again. But if that person is poisoned and despicable, the dirt will never depart from him, for the soiling is compounded with the previous soiling.

MAN UNITES CREATION

2:7. And He blew into his nose the soul of life.

Rashi: He made him of the lower world and of the upper world, his soul from the upper and his body from the lower. On the first day, He created heaven and earth; on the second, the firmament for the upper; on the third, the dry land appeared for the lower; on the fourth, the luminaries for the upper; on the fifth, the waters swarmed for the lower; and, on the sixth, He needed to create for both [the upper and the lower] or else there would be jealousy in creation.

Gur Arye: The blowing of the soul of life is more than that which occurred in the creation of other living things. "From the earth" [2:7] means from the lower world. The blowing of the soul of life is from the upper world. The jealousy between the worlds derives from imbalance, as the midrash notes [BR 1:15], at times heaven precedes earth [1:1] and at times earth precedes heaven [2:4] to teach us that they are equal to each other. The meaning of jealousy is imbalance.

AN INVITATION TO THE GARDEN

2:17. And Hashem Elokim took the man and put
him in the Garden of Eden.

Rashi: He took him with pleasant words and persuaded him to enter.

Gur Arye: Physical "taking" does not apply to man, for the main, principal character of man is that he is *maskil* [spiritual, intelligent] and the physical taking of a spiritual being does not apply. Even if one takes the body of a person into one's domain, one cannot take his soul or his mind. To say He took him with words, that He convinced him, fits man's spiritual and intellectual status.[61] Wherever "taking" is mentioned with reference to people, Rashi explains it that someone appealed to that person with words.[62]

---

61. In discussing the Waters of Strife [Num. 20:12], Gur Arye notes that had Moshe spoken to the rock, Israel would have seen that all things that exist, even inanimate ones, are drawn to Hashem and His word. They "act" on their own account and not because of coercion. Therefore Moshe was told to speak to the rock. Then the rock's giving out water would be out of willingness and happiness, a real sanctification of His name. See also Gevurot Hashem 7:44a.

62. 16:3: "Sarai took Hagar…and gave her to Avram." Rashi: She persuaded her by telling her that she would be privileged to cleave to such a holy body. Ex. 14:6: "Paro took his nation with him." Rashi: He drew them forth with words – "Let us strike them and take back our property." Lev. 8:2: "Take Aharon…" Rashi: Take him with words and draw him out. Num. 8:6: "Take the Leviim…" Rashi: Take them with words – "You will be fortunate to merit being the personal servants of the Omnipresent." Num. 11:16: "Gather to me seventy men…and you will take them…" Rashi: Take them with words – "You are fortunate to be appointed sustainers of the children of the Omnipresent." Num. 20:25: "Take Ahron and his son, Elazar, and bring them up to Hor mountain…" Rashi: With words of consolation – "You are fortunate to see your crown given to your son, which I do not merit." Num. 27:18: "Take to you Yehoshua bin Nun…" Rashi: Take him with words – "You are fortunate to lead the children of the Omnipresent." Deut. 1:15: "And I took the heads of your tribes…" Rashi: I persuaded them verbally – "You are fortunate! Over whom do you come to

Now it fits that He also took man's *da'at* [knowledge, mind, disposition] with his permission, with words. He persuaded him so that this "taking" would be with man's *da'at* – this is the main principle of his being human – his *da'at* and his *sechel* [spirituality, intelligence]. Thus, man's free will was established in his first interaction with his Creator.

MDK: Onkelos translates vayikach [he took] *as* unesaiv *if the object of the verb is other than human, and* udvar [he spoke] *if the object is human. Two exceptions prove the rule – Eliezer took his camels* [14:10] *not physically, but by coaxing* [udvar], *and a man taking a wife* [Deut. 22:15], *which is rendered by Onkelos as* unesaiv [takes], *for marriage is strictly business.*

---

be appointed? Over the sons of Avraham, Yitzchak, and Yaakov, people called "brothers" [Ps. 122:8], "friends" [Prov. 27:10], a "portion and an inheritance of Hashem" [Deut. 32:9] and all expressions of endearment." Rashi elaborates on the meaning of "taking" in his comment on *Bereshit* 43:15, "And the men took this tribute, and they took double money in their hand, and Binyamin..." Rashi: Targum Onkelos uses two separate verbs. For the tribute and the money he renders "took" as *v'nasvu*, while for Binyamin, he renders the verb *udvaru yas Binyamin*, because taking money and taking a person do not use the same verb in Aramaic. A thing taken in the hand is translated *unesaiv*, but a thing or person taken by being led by words is translated *udvar*. Here Hashem's first interaction with man was respectful of, and indeed established the principle of, man's free will.

THE PROBLEMATIC COUPLING OF OPPOSITES

2:18. I will make him a helper against him.

Rashi: If he is zoche *[fortunate, worthy], she is a helper. If not, she is against him, to wage war.*

Gur Arye: The simple explanation is a helper in opposition, different from the helping relationship between father and son in which there is no opposition. Here, the help is in opposition, for the woman is important and equal to the man.[63] The woman aids the man, as the man brings and the wife fixes.[64] That is what a "helper *kenegdo*" [opposite him, corresponding to him] means.[65] Therefore, if he is not *zoche* she is in complete opposition to him, as Rashi says, "to wage war."[66] Another aspect is that male and female are opposites, and if he is *zoche*, they become connected together in a single force, for all opposites unite when they are *zoche*. That is to say, that Hashem, may He be blessed, makes *shalom* [peace, harmony, completeness] – He ties them together[67] and

---

63. Be'er Hagola 6:108b: For his wife enters in opposition to the man – he is called *adam* [man] only along with his wife, as it says [5:2]: "He created them male and female...and called their name *adam.*" Gevurot Hashem 68:314b: Woman is also within the category of man because the male is not "man" without the female, and the two together are *adam* [man, human].

64. Yeb. 63a: How does she help him? He brings in wheat kernels – does he bite down on wheat kernels? He brings in raw flax – does he wear raw flax? [Without her] he has no light in his eye or standing on his legs.

65. Be'er Hagola 5:96b: *Kenegdo* means like him, equal to him. See *Gevurot Hashem* 19:87a.

66. See Pirke Derabbi Eliezer 12.

67. Be'er Hagola 4:83a. Gevurot Hashem 43:163a: Discord is a physical thing and unity is Godly. See also Tiferet Yisrael 30:90b. See also Netiv Hashalom 1, 1:215a about making peace between opposites.

connects them.[68] But when they lack this *zechut* [*worthiness, good fortune*], the fact that they are opposites results in strife.

In fact, the coupling of humans could not occur in nature! The opposing and equal forces of the male and the female would preclude their union [Be'er Hagola, 4:83a]. Certainly, they can couple on a *gufani* [physical, bodily, animal] level, but on the level of *nefesh* [soul, spirit], the essence of the male and female are in opposition to the point that they repel one another. Only by elevating themselves toward the spiritual do they merit the involvement of Hashem coming between them to unite the two supernal souls. This is the message of the Talmud [Sot. 17a]: In *ish* [*alef, yud, shin*; man] and *isha* [*alef, shin, heh*; woman], is Hashem's name *Yah* [*yud, heh*], for He connects them. Removal of *Yah* from *ish* and *isha* leaves *aish* [fire] and *aish*.

MDK: Although it may be the commonalities of the man and the woman that attracted them to each other in the first place, it is the accommodation to their differences that is the bedrock of a successful marriage. This, with Hashem's help, is the peace between opposites.

---

68. Chidushei Agadot on Yeb. 63a, 1:135b: When opposites unite in a single *koach* [power, potential], He ties and connects them. This needs *zechut* [good fortune, worthiness] from on High, for by way of *zechut* man is exalted and the connection and the cleaving is from above, for the lower world is filled with discord and strife.

Addenda

WHY THE WORLD WAS CREATED

1:1. In the beginning [of] *Elokim* created heaven
and earth.

*Rashi: This verse says nothing but "expound me." The Rabbis of
blessed memory expounded: On account of Torah which is* called
*"the beginning of His way" [Prov. 8:22], and on account of Israel who
is called "the first of His crop" [Jer. 2:3].*

Gur Arye: Rashi, tracking the footprints of the midrash [BR 1:4]
through the dark forest of the Torah's account of creation, is troubled by the Torah's opening word, *bereshit*. The terminal *tav* signals that the word must be connected to the word following and
means "of." As the following word in this case is a verb, the dan-
gling preposition, "of," needs to be explained. Rashi does explain,
telling us here the reason why Hashem created the world.

First, let us consider why Hashem should create anything.
It is written, "All work of Hashem is for Himself" [Prov. 16:4],
meaning everything in the world was created for the Holy One,
blessed be He, and His Glory [Yom. 38a]. "Everything is called in
My Name – I created it for My Glory" [Isa. 43:7].[1] His Glory flows

---

1.   Maharal, Gevurot Hashem 68:314a: The purpose of all Hashem's creation is to
     honor Him, and therefore all creatures say *shira* [songs of praise] to the The Holy
     One, blessed be He, for *shira* is His glory and everything that exists has some

from creatures when they fulfill His commands and serve Him.[2] With respect to the Jewish nation,[3] it is said, "This nation I created for Me, they will tell My praise[4] [Isa. 43:21] and Israel serves The Holy One, blessed be He, only by His commandments.[5]

---

of His glory…" Also note Be'er Hagola 4:65b and 5:104a and Derech Hachaim 1, 2:276 and 6, 10:320 and Derasha Leshabbat Hagadol 193b: All creations were created for His sake. A person should not think that the praise of the Creator of all does not emanate from small things like the swarming animals – just the opposite, consider that even the existence of such a creature sings His praise.

2. Maharal, Derasha Leshabbat Hagadol: The beginning of man's creation and the purpose of his life is to serve his Creator. Even when he eats and drinks to sustain himself, since the inception of his creation is for His honor, the eating and drinking and survival in and of themselves can be said to be thus created to honor Hashem, as everything is for The Holy One, may His Name be blessed."

3. Maharal, Be'er Hagolah 4:65b: All creation was for Hashem's glory. Glory has two aspects. First, the King has glory for he has great important officers close to him and they are His and for His glory, and the second, that he rules and reigns over all, even those distant from him. Hashem's glory from Israel is from the first aspect. Derech Hachayim 6, 10:321a: The explanation of the verse in Isaiah, "All are called in My name and in My honor" – 'called in My name' refers to the righteous, called in the name of The Holy One, blessed be He [B.B. 75b]: just like the Holy One, blessed be He is called kadosh [holy, apart, elevated] the righteous are called kadosh. In that way the righteous are called by the name of the Holy One, blessed be He. Likewise see Chidushei Agadot on Baba Batra 75b [3:115a].

4. Maharal, Ner Mitzva 8a: This nation was created to glorify The Holy One, may His Name be blessed, as it is written [Prov. 8:22], "I created this nation to praise Me." Even if the four kingdoms [Yishmael, Edom, Moav, Amon] increased His glory in this lower world, and they gave honor to His name, Hashem would not desire their honey or their sting. For the essence of His glory is that He is One in His world and there is none else beside Him – this means the nations diminish, and they were not created for this – only Israel which is a singular nation, as the verse hints, "This nation I created…." The word zo [this] has a numeric value of 13, which is the equivalent of echad [one]. [The verse is then read as saying], This nation testifies that Hashem is One. The idea that Israel represents the secret of oneness with respect to the nations of the world who represent multitude is cited in Netzach Yisrael 32:159a, Gevurot Hashem 69:318a and Netiv Ha'avoda1, 1:78b.

5. Maharal, Netzach Yisrael 10:61a: "Who is like your nation, Israel, a singular nation" [Sam. II 7:23] for they have the Torah, and because of that they are

Rashi quotes these two, Torah and Israel, even though the Rabbis have expounded many matters for which the world was created.[6] The world was created on account of Torah. In the beginning of everything was the Torah, which was created 2000 years before the world [BR 8:2], and nothing was created last but Israel, for no creation occurred after Israel. Edom and Moav were created as nations before Israel, and Israel later.[7]

The Torah is the first of all creation, for from it all was designed,[8] like the oak which, having been planted, only grows on account of the part [the acorn] which is its origin. But the purpose of its growth is to give out fruit, and on this account it grows and flowers. Likewise Israel, who came out last of all creations, harmoniously completed the whole world and creation stood, for it had reached its purpose and its *shelemut* [harmonious completion, perfection].

Therefore, the world was created on account of Torah, which was the initial conception and blueprint, and on account of Israel, which is the purpose of it all. Israel is called *reshit* [beginning] [Jer. 2:3] for the purpose was in the inception of the thought.[9] This

---

a singular nation. About Torah it is written [Num. 15:29]: "You will have one Torah, and by way of the Torah, Israel will also be a single nation." See also Derech Hachaim 6: 10,320b.

6. Mizrachi: Avraham, Moshe, first fruits, tithes, and *chala* are all mentioned as other reasons for Creation.

7. Maharal, Chidushei Agadot on Men. 53b [4:62b]. There were seventy nations in the generation of dispersion, and Amon and Moav became nations before Israel, for Israel came in to actuality when they came out of Egypt. Israel was commanded to circumvent their land, for Hashem had given them their land as an inheritance first [Deut. 2:5,1,18]. If so, the nations comprise two groups, the 70 nations from the generation of dispersion and the four nations related to Avraham: Yishmael, Amon, Moav, and Edom. See Gur Arye, Deut. 2:9, Tiferet Yisrael 12:42b, ibid 17:55a, Gevurot Hashem 2:114a and 69:316b, Netzach Yisrael 10:61b, and others.

8. BR 1:1: The Holy One, blessed be He, looked into the Torah and created the world. See Netivot Torah 1, 1:3–4 and Gevurot Hashem 70:220b.

9. Alkabetz, Lecha Dodi: "The final act was in the original thought." See Gur Arye 37:3[16].

will clarify that which the Sages said of Israel [Yeb. 61a], "You are called Man," for Israel is compared to Man in that all living things were created first and then Man, i.e., Man completed the whole,[10] like the nations were created first and Israel last.[11] These words are secret and most wondrous. Rashi has turned the terminal *tav* into the secret of why the world was created.

MDK: This selection was the first that endeared Maharal to me and drew me into the project, the fruit of which is this work. My emotional attachment to it blinded me to the difficulties the reader would encounter if he opened the book to this as the first selection. It is hard to read because it must be learned and analyzed, and I intended the book to be attractive to the layman as well as the scholar. I felt the footnotes were very important, but I couldn't incorporate them into the text as I did throughout the book because the text itself was so difficult. My uncle, a psychiatrist and independent thinker, stopped me cold with, "What does He need honor for? The God I believe in is sufficiently secure and self assured that He doesn't need honor, let alone to create a world just to get it!" I then realized that kavod must mean something other than honor, but have been unsuccessful in my quest to find a meaning that fits, even after consulting my mentors and other great rabbinic minds. Then there is the issue of chosenness, which grates against the sensibilities of anyone brought up on the Jeffersonian concept of all men being created equal. After more than thirty years of serious pursuit of Torah, I can assert with pride that I am a member of Hashem's chosen people, but this book is written for both the learned and the

---

10. Maharal, Derashah Leshabbat Hagadol [174–5]: Man was created last for he completed the act of creation. Man united the world, for the upper and lower spheres were apart, and Man who was created from both [Rashi: 1:2, 1:7] connected and united the upper and lower spheres. Therefore Man was made last.

11. See Gur Arye, Numb. 31:19, Netzach Yisrael 14:63c, and Ner Mitzvah 10a.

uninitiated, and this selection is not the one that should greet the reader on page one. I therefore made an addendum containing selections that require learning and not just reading.

RABBI YITZCHAK'S QUESTION

1:1. In the beginning *Elokim* created the heaven and the earth.

Rashi: Rabbi Yitzchak said: The Torah need not to have begun until the first commandment given to Israel, that is [Ex. 12:2] "This month shall be for you the beginning of months..." Why begin with Genesis? Because God [Ps. 111:6] "told His people the power of His acts in order to give them the estate of nations," so that if the nations of the world will say to Israel, 'You are bandits for conquering the land of the seven nations,' Israel will answer, 'The whole world belongs to the Holy One, blessed be He. He created it and gave it to whomever He saw fit.'

Gur Arye: Why does Rebbe Yitzchak in his question [BR 1:2] assume Torah to be synonymous with the commandments?[12] The word, Torah, means teaching[13] and its purpose is to teach us the deeds we ought to do.[14] If so, why call it Torah instead of *mitzvot* [commandments]? Because the latter term connotes the intent of the commander to have the command carried out irrespective of the knowledge and intent of the one commanded. When Hashem gives the commandments to Israel, He wants Israel to know and understand the whys and wherefores as well as the wisdom contained in them, and to observe them with this knowledge. This is called Torah,[15] and it teaches man the path to reach his ultimate purpose, the World to Come.[16]

Why does Rabbi Yitzchak in his answer assume the com-

---

12. See Sanh. 99b.
13. R. David Kimche, Sefer Hashorashim [Book of Roots], *yud-resh-heh*.
14. Zohar 3:53b: Why is it called Torah? Because it illuminates and reveals that which is secret and unknown.
15. See Be'er Hagola 50b.
16. See Netiv Hatorah 1, 1:4a and Tiferet Yisrael 9:32b and Derech Hachaim 3:23, 159a.

mandments to be synonymous with the Land of Israel? Why is giving the Land of Israel to the people of Israel an introduction to the mitzvot of the Torah? The answer is that most of the mitzvot are dependent on the Land.[17] Ramban even wrote that all the mitzvot of the Torah belong specifically in the Land![18] Thus the inheritance of the Land is a prerequisite to the Torah and its commandments.

MDK: The implicit assumptions in the Rashi are drawn out as messages by Gur Arye. The terms Torah *and* mitzvot [commandments] *refer to the same thing, and* mitzvot *and the Land of Israel are likewise inseparable.*

---

17. Sot. 14a: Why did Moshe our teacher so strongly desire to enter the Land of Israel? Because many of the *mitzvot* that Israel was commanded are fulfilled in the Land of Israel.
18. Ramban, Gen. 26:5 and Lev. 18:25.

LESSON IN HUMILITY

1:26. And God said: "Let us make man…"

Rashi: Though the angels did not assist in man's creation, this phrase opens the door for heretics to claim multiple deities took part. Nevertheless, the Torah did not refrain from teaching proper behavior and the trait of humility, that the greater one should consult and take permission from the lesser one. Had it written, "I shall make man," we would not have learned that He was speaking with His court and not to Himself. To rebut the heretics, the next verse is in the singular – "And He created man." We learn from here the humility of the Holy One, blessed be He, for man resembles the angels and they would be jealous of him, so He consults with them. When He judges kings, He consults His heavenly court, as we find with Achav. Micha said to him, "I have seen God sitting on His throne with all the host of heaven standing right and left [Kings 1 22:19]." Are there right and left before Him? Right means seeking to declare innocent and left means seeking to declare guilty…Here too He consulted His retinue and took their permission.

Gur Arye: The judgment of kings is the biblical paradigm for instances in which Hashem consults with the angels. Why kings and not other creatures? Kings are important and judging them is a major undertaking. Lesser undertakings, like other creatures, do not require consultation. Notwithstanding, when it came to the creation of man, He did consult the angels.

Rashi explains why Hashem did so. The first reason is to teach us humility. Before He undertakes His ultimate creation, the reason for creation altogether, He incorporates an earlier creation, the Heavenly Court, into the process. Humility is an intermediate quality between arrogance and lowliness, and one should not lower one's self esteem more than that which is proper,[19] which

---

19. However, it must be pointed out that Rambam set down in Mishne Torah, Laws of Ethics 2:5: It is not a good way that man should be humble, but he

would have been the case had He consulted the angels about the creation of, say, the ant. Likewise the rabbis[20] and Rambam in the fourth chapter of the Eight Chapters affirm this. Therefore He asks advice about a matter that involves humility to teach us humility. A second reason is that the angels not be jealous. For the lesson of humility alone He would not have needed their advice, but on account of the jealousy factor He consulted them. This is why Rashi develops both ideas.

This disagrees with Sanhedrin 38b: The Holy One, blessed be He, does nothing till He consults His retinue. A human king may act and his act may be right for him but not for another king, for all kings do not think alike.[21] But the works of Hashem are right and true for all circumstances and all minds. He consults His angels for all His acts and His deeds are right and true for all of them. Why, then, is such consultation mentioned with respect to the creation of man? The answer is that it speaks to the importance of man. For all creation depended on man [the Anthropic Principle]. For man to be created, the rest of creation was required, and all of it was to serve man.[22]

---

should be of lowly spirit to the extreme. Therefore Moshe was 'humble to the extreme' [Num. 12:3]. Also Ab. 4:4: Be of very, very lowly spirit. See Gur Arye on Lev. 14:4[3].

20. Sot. 5b: All who set their ways [establish their attitudes with intention] in this world will merit seeing the salvation of the Holy One, blessed be He. Rambam, Laws of Ethics 1:4: The early sages commanded that a person should always establish his attitudes and rein them in and direct them to the path of moderation. Kesef Mishne points out that the source for this view is Sota 5b.

21. Tanchuma, Pinchas 10: Just as their faces are not the same, their thoughts are not the same. And in contrast to Rashi who says that the angels did not assist in the creation of man, Gevurot Hashem 67:311a says: Let us make man – let us consult with the angels. This teaches us that all the angels are heavenly powers – seventy corresponding to the seventy nations – all were partners in man.

22. Rashi 6:7: All was created on man's account, based on Sanh. 108a. Likewise BR 28:6, Kid. 82a, Derech Hachaim 5:1, 217b and Be'er Hagola 4:58b. See N. Aviezer, Fossils and Faith, Ch. 3.

MDK: I was tempted to trim this selection down to the humility lesson, but I decided the question from Sanhedrin 38a was worthy of inclusion. This is a rare example of Gur Aryeh's rejection of an explanation offered by Rashi, and he does it for two reasons. First, Rashi invokes humility and jealousy as reasons to consult the Heavenly Court, for neither suffices on its own. Secondly, Rashi fails to deal with a more reliable source in the gemara. *Since it must be studied and not just read, I moved it to the addenda.*

MAN – THE CATALYST FOR
HARMONY IN THE UNIVERSE

Rashi: [continued from previous Rashi] If My likeness would be absent from the lower world there would be jealousy in creation.

Gur Arye: Jealousy only applies to beings possessing *sechel* [intelligence, spirituality]. How could the beings of the lower world before man was created be jealous? The answer is jealousy occurs if there is inequality between upper and lower worlds. The requirement of equality derives from balanced verses, one with heaven preceding earth [1:1], the other vice versa [2:4]. Man was thus created from both worlds [Rashi 2:7], the dust of the earth and the life force Hashem blew into his nostrils. This was in order that there not be jealousy. This is a secret from the secret parts of the Torah, for heaven and earth must be tied together, as Rambam explains in Guide to the Perplexed 1:2. Man unites the upper and lower worlds.[23] Jealousy means separation and opposition deriving from the inequality. It is proper that man was created to make *shalom* [harmony, completion, perfection] between the worlds and unite all, as man has the form and image of the Holy One, blessed be He.

---

23. Derech Hachaim 1:18[58a], and 5:15[254b], Chidushei Agadot on Sanh. 38a, 3:148b, and Derasha Leshabbat Hagadol 195a.

Book II: The Fall of Man: 2000 Years of Tohu

THE CURSE OF CHAVA

> 3:16. To the woman He said, I will much increase
> your suffering and your pregnancy; in pain you
> shall bear children…

Rashi: "Your suffering" is the pain of raising children, "your pregnancy" is the pain of your pregnancy, and the "pain of bearing children" is labor pains.

Gur Arye: Rashi is quoting *Eruvin* [100b]. Bereshit Rabba, however, interprets "suffering" to mean the pain of the menses of a woman. The latter is a more logical sequence – menses, then pregnancy, then labor, as it occurs in the life cycle of a woman. Rashi does not bring this midrash because it violates a cardinal principle – Hashem, may He be blessed, does not bring upon a person something that has only negative consequences to the individual,[24] like menstrual bleeding which has no positive purpose or favorable outcome. Raising children, like pregnancy and the delivery that follows, are good things that Hashem gives us by way of pain and suffering.

Hashem, through His Attribute of Goodness, desires that the world be good, therefore He brings retribution to the world to pay off the evildoers. The evil then departs from the world and [only] good remains…Because He is good, He wants good…Even the bad He brings to the world is brought only because of His Goodness. Menses do not fit this model.

---

24. Maharal, Derech Hachaim 149b, on 3:15, on "the world is judged in goodness." See also Netiv Gemilut Chasadim 1, 1:150a and Gur Arye on Moshe's authorship of the curses in Deut. 28:23: This explains why there are no words of consolation at the end of the curses, for the suffering Hashem brings about is ultimately good, for no bad thing comes from Him. That is why there is consolation at the end of the curses in Leviticus, where Hashem "hides His Face," but not here.

MDK: Rashi capitalizes on his terseness to select the message he wants to convey. He prefers a theologic message that teaches us one of Hashem's "rules of conduct" to a message that has no theologic content but is more in tune with observed reality.

If Rashi's Eruvin midrash is correct and BR is incorrect, Maharal would be left with the problem of menses, which serves no positive purpose. Maharal does not posit there is no bad thing in the world, for that goes against Yeshayah's "Creator of evil" description of God [Isa. 45:7]. The latter may refer to nature, which operates by different rules, as Gur Arye will discuss in Exod. 15:26. Alternatively, both midrashim may be correct.

IS THIS A CURSE?

> 3:16. Your yearning shall be for your husband....

Rashi: This yearning is for sexual intimacy. Nevertheless you will not have the brazenness to lay claim to it verbally. He shall rule over you, for the initiation of the conjugal act will come from him and not you.

Gur Arye: What kind of a curse is this? *Teshuka* [desire, yearning] is a good thing that leads to pleasure and offspring! Another question is the part of her curse that he shall dominate her – this was previously established [Rashi 1:28] in the command, "be fruitful and multiply and fill the earth *v'chivshuha* [and conquer it]. The latter word is missing the second *vav* and appears as *v'chovshah* [and he shall conquer her] commanding him to rein her in so that she not be a gadabout. Why state it again as a curse here? Rashi answers both of these questions. The curse is that her *teshuka* is unanswered unless he reciprocates. The mechanics of intimacy require his arousal and active participation. His dominance stands in the way of the fulfillment of her sexual yearning.

MDK: Maharal's genius is in comprehending human nature and seeing timeless truth reflected in his understanding of the words of the sages.

THE THIRD SISTER

> 4:1–2. She gave birth to [*et*] Kayin…and she continued and gave birth to [*et*] his brother, [*et*] Hevel.

Rashi: Three etim [untranslated words that connote objects of transitive verbs and are usually interpreted to expand their meaning] teach that Kayin was born with a twin sister and Hevel with two triplet sisters.

Gur Arye: In order to harmoniously complete seven people to correspond to the seven days of creation,[25] a third female sibling was required. Mankind is equal to the whole world, that is, all seven days of Creation.[26] Before the second female triplet of Hevel was considered, there would have been three males and three females partnered to the days, as the rabbis said [BR 11:9]: "Shabbat said before the Holy One, blessed be He, 'You gave all the days partners

---

25. Adam, Chava, Kayin, Hevel, and three female twins. *Baba Batra* 121b: Seven people's lives overlapped so as to cover the entire duration of the world. Metushelach saw Adam, Shem saw Metushelach, Yaakov saw Shem, Amram saw Yaakov, Achiya Hashiloni saw Eliahu, and Eliahu still lives. Maharal explains in Chidushei Agadot, 3:124b: This world was created in the seven days of Creation. It is proper that seven include the duration of the world from beginning to end, for man is considered as one day, for all the sixth day was drawn after his creation, as the rabbis said [Sanh. 37a]: The first hour He gathered dust etc. [see 2:7[19]{51}] and you will find the seven days of Creation include the entire world [see Ramban on 2:3]. That is how seven people overlap to include the whole world.
26. 2:23[42]{126}: Man is considered the *tzura* [spiritual character] of the world. Derech Hachaim on 3:2, 114a: Man is the *tzura* of the world, therefore one person is considered a whole world. Just as man is equal to the "space" of the world, he is equal to the "time" of the world, for space equals time. Tiferet Yisrael 27: 79a: Space and time are one continuum. Derasha al Hatorah, 23b: Space and time belong and relate to each other, as space is on the earth and time depends on the array of the heavens and their orbits.

but me.'"[27] There needed to be another female along with Hevel to correspond to Shabbat."[28] Know that Shabbat is always female, called "bride" and "queen"[29] [B.K. 32b], and "He who profanes her shall surely die" [Ex. 31:14].

MDK: Gur Arye merges Rashi's midrash with the midrash of Shabbat's complaint.

27. Tiferet Yisrael 40:123b and Derech Hachaim 14b.
28. Gur Arye 35:17[12]: As every ending is a harmonious completion, Binyamin, the last, harmoniously completed the twelve tribes along with an extra twin sister, for the female harmoniously completes the person. Hevel also had two triplet sisters for this reason.
29. Chidushei Agadot on B.K. 32b, 3:5b and Tiferet Yisrael 40:123b.

WHY KAYIN WAS A FARMER

4:2. Hevel was a shepherd, and Kayin had been
a worker of the earth.

*Rashi: Because the earth was cursed, Hevel separated himself from
it so as not to work on it.*

Gur Arye: Otherwise, why should Hevel not be a farmer? Animal
husbandry was of limited value, for Hashem had forbidden the
eating of meat until Noach [Rashi 1:29], and the only benefits were
milk and wool. Farming, then, was more important but also more
degrading [Yeb. 63a]. Why was Kayin not a shepherd? As firstborn, he had his choice of occupations. One answer is he needed
to work the land because producing food is the first thing man
must do to live. It is impossible to sustain oneself on milk and
wool. That is why Kayin had already been [*haya* in scripture is the
pluperfect "had been"] a farmer when Hevel chose his occupation.[30]
Another answer is that "an evil soul desires evil"[31] [Prov. 21:10]
and Kayin's soul was wicked, as witnessed by his poor choice of
sacrifice. Therefore he desired that which was cursed – the earth.
That is the way of the world – the good desire the good and the
wicked desire the not good.[32]

---

30. That which is necessary precedes that which is desirable, and obligatory matters precede optional matters. See Gur Arye on Deut. 5:17 and Ex. 30:15, and
Pachad Yitzchak, Pesach 44:1.

31. Derech Hachaim, intro., 9a: No person attains good or benefit from injuring
his neighbor…if one hurts another with his hands – this is an evil soul, as it
is written, "The evil soul desires evil…" [Prov. 21:10]. …someone wicked in
his essence desires something wicked in its essence, even if he gets no benefit
from it. Only on account of his wickedness is he attracted to evil.

32. Netiv Hayetzer 4, 2:130b: In the midrash [BR 20:7] there are four *teshukot*
[desires, yearnings]…the *teshuka* of the evil inclination for Kayin and his
friends, the *teshuka* of the Holy One, blessed be He is only for Israel. The evil
inclination cleaves to the wicked, for evil attaches to him who is prepared for
it…Hashem who is complete Good has a *teshuka* for that which is good and

MDK: The midrash of the occupations is based on the difference in tense – Hevel was…and Kayin had been…Of the two explanations, the first is practical – the firstborn did what needed to be done, i.e., grow the food for the first family. The second is metaphysical – since the received wisdom is "like is attracted to like," Kayin, whose nature is evil, is drawn to the accursed earth.

---

cleaves to it. That is how *teshuka* works – the good loves the good and the bad loves the bad. See 1:11[33]<112>.

THE UNACCEPTED GIFT

4:3. And Kayin brought a gift to Hashem from
the fruit of the earth.

Rashi: From the poorest – there is a midrash that it was flaxseed.

Gur Arye: Rashi learns this from "from the fruit" instead of "the fruit," meaning partial and separate from other fruit, i.e., the poorest. In contrast, Hevel's offering was "of the firstlings of his flock" [4:4] – certainly here the "of" means the best of.[33] Now we must understand why Kayin, who had the opportunity to bring any of the fruits of the earth as his offering,[34] should take the poorest. It certainly was not that he was miserly or wanted the best for himself. It appears that a person accomplishes his goal within the limit of his *koach* [potential, power], and Kayin's *koach* was his evil eye.[35] He understood his own character and brought an offering in an attempt to credit and strengthen his cause – that of evil. Kayin planned his offering considering that on account of it he would be acceptable to Hashem. However, the offering of the wicked like this is an abomination, and He did not accept the gift. Kayin's intent was to have his poor and wicked gift accepted,

---

33. Nachalat Ya'akov here: The use of the *mem* indicates partial, as it says in Berachot 50a: "In His Goodness we live" – this is a wise scholar, "Of His Goodness [*mitovato*] we live" – this is a boor. Rashi explains: "of His Goodness" minimizes the gift of the Omnipresent. By Hevel, "of the firstlings" might mean the poorest of the firstlings, were it not for "and their fat ones" which assures that the *mem* means the best. Rashi 45:18: All fat means best.

34. Rashi, Lev. 1:2: Adam never brought an offering which was stolen, for all was his.

35. Derech Hachaim on 4:22, 207a: Adam had two sons. One, Hevel, had the *koach* of lust, and the other, Kayin, had the *koach* of jealousy. Kayin was jealous of Hevel when the gift of the latter was accepted by Hashem. He is called Kayin on account of his *kina* [jealousy]. Netiv Hayetzer 1, 2:211b: Jealousy is in the heart, for one who has an evil heart is jealous whenever his friend has something good.

implying Hashem's acceptance of his own wickedness.[36] By this he would overcome his brother and gain acceptance by Hashem in spite of his evil nature and deeds.However, as Hashem is Good [Men. 53b], He turns to the good and not to the evil.

With respect to the choice of flaxseed, Mizrachi notes that *mincha* [gift, gift offering] means *korban* [sacrifice, offering]. If each letter is spelled out the way it is pronounced the last letters are *kuf, resh, bet, nun – pishtan* [flax]. But he fails to note another connection, that Kayin the farmer and Hevel the shepherd would each bring a sacrifice from that which belonged to him, to increase his own *koach* at the expense of that of his brother.[37] The product Kayin grew that most differentiated and separated him from his brother's wool was his flax, for linen and wool cannot mix.[38] Kayin's gift was specifically his, as Hevel and his wool could not be associated with it. Kayin and Hevel were opposites[39] who could not exist together.[40] When Shet was born, he was the foundation

---

36. Derasha Leshabbat Hagadol 202a.

37. Derasha Leshabbat Hagadol 201a: Adam had three sons and three behaviors. Wicked deeds from the evil inclination in man, vain [*hevel*] deeds that are neither good nor wicked, and good deeds, were all committed by Adam. Correspondingly, the first son, Kayin, had the evil inclination; the second son, Hevel, was connected to vain, meaningless deeds; and the third son, Shet, was connected to good deeds. The name Shet means "foundation" as in *even shetia* [foundation stone]. Understand that Hevel cared for animals which could not be used for food, a meaningless activity that corresponded to his trait. Kayin worked the earth, the source of sin, corresponding to his trait, for the earth is physical, and sin is associated with it.

38. See Deut. 22:11.

39. Derech Hachaim on 4:22, 207a: Just as lust and jealousy cannot endure, neither Kayin nor Hevel could endure in the world. Lust is from the *guf* [body devoid of soul] and jealousy from *nefesh* [body combined with soul], and both lack eternal endurance.

40. Gur Arye 25:22[26]: Yaakov and Esav cannot be partners together in the world for they in their essence are in opposition to each other. That is why they could not coexist in their mother's womb, a single space they were forced to share in spite of their mutual opposition, like fire and water. See Netzach Yisrael 15:87b.

of all humanity.[41] These are the words of the sages [Tanchuma, Bereshit 9] who said Kayin brought flaxseed. Blessed is He who chose them and their wisdom [Ab. 6:1].

If Hevel brought a proper offering, why did Hashem not protect him? Why did he have to die? The answer is that he too was at fault. His offering, a sheep, was intended to oppose and upstage Kayin's offering. He could have brought an ox, as did his father Adam, as described in the Gemara.[42] Hashem saw fit not to protect Hevel[43] because his intention was to distance Kayin further from His blessing, not to actually honor Hashem. That is why it is written, "And Hevel **also** brought..." [4:4] – his offering was a response to Kayin's. This answers an earlier question – why did Kayin take pains to bring a poor gift? He wanted to do the opposite of his brother. His brother the shepherd would bring what he

---

41. Num. R. 14:12. Footnote 37 continued: Shet corresponds to the third *koach*, the *sichli* [spiritual] – Maharal uses this term interchangibly with *neshama hanivdal* {soul disassociated from body, a higher level than *guf* and *nefesh*}, not comparable to the other two lesser *kochot*]. This son, Shet, was more connected to Hashem. Hashem brought the potential *sechel* into actuality. Note Gur Arye 9:23[17] comparing Noach's three sons to Adam's three sons.

42. A.Z. 8a: Adam sinned on the day he was created. When the sun set, he lamented: Woe is me! Because of my sin the world is doomed to return to darkness and chaos. This must be the death penalty ordained for me. Adam and Chava wept bitterly through the night but were mollified the next morning when the sun rose. As winter approached, the days became shorter, and Adam feared that this was how Hashem would punish him and return the world to darkness and chaos. He fasted eight days, the winter solstice passed, and the days began to lengthen. Adam celebrated by declaring a holiday on which he sacrificed a fully grown bullock.

43. Derasha Leshabbat Hagadol 202a: Some ask why, if Hashem accepted Hevel's gift, was he not protected, as "he who keeps a commandment did not know an evil thing" [Prov. 19:16]. The answer is hinted at in the word "also." He saw that Kayin offered a gift, so he had to do the same. The deeds of such a jealous person are empty, as Shlomo said, "I saw all the hard work and effort done on account of jealousy that one person has for another – this is also vanity and badness of spirit" [Eccl. 4:4].

had, the fat and the good,[44] and he, who farmed the cursed earth,[45] correspondingly offered the poor, the opposite of Hevel.

MDK: A recurrent theme in the works of Maharal is the three-part nature of man. The guf *is the body, the purely physical and material aspect of man. The* nefesh *is that part of his spiritual nature which is attached to his* guf. *The* neshama, *also called the* sechel hanivdal [detached spirit], *refers to the pure, supernal soul.*

---

44. Continuation of footnote 37: Hevel's attribute was desire; therefore his offering was good to eat.
45. Continuation of footnote 37: Kayin was a farmer, befitting his character. If he would plant fruit, "thorns and thistles would sprout" [3:18] – the earth would change its *koach* for which it was created and bring forth thorns. Likewise man, created with the *koach* to do good deeds which are called "good fruit" [Kid. 40a] can change his *koach* and bring forth thistles and thorns.

THE UNIFYING THEORY OF SIN

4:7. But if you do not do good, sin crouches at
the door. Its yearning is for you, but you must
conquer it.

Rashi: At the entrance to your grave, your sin is preserved.

Gur Arye: Rashi takes "door" to mean the opening to your grave.
However, Targum Onkelos translates the phrase as "till the day of
judgment, sin is preserved," which seems to mean that a person's
sins lie in wait till his death, then present themselves for recom-
pense. Onkelos further renders "its longing is for you" – it [sin]
will take payment from you in the future. Rashi and Onkelos are
reconciled if sin, the evil inclination, and the Angel of Death are
understood to be one and the same. The Talmud states [B.B. 16a]:
"He descends, causes man to err, ascends, prosecutes, takes permission, then snatches the soul." Rashi explains that he descends to
earth, entraps people in sin, then ascends and arouses the anger of
the King, and takes from Him permission to kill the sinner. "He"
is at once the sin, the Satan, the evil inclination, the prosecutor,
and the Angel of Death.

*MDK: In this verse, Hashem reveals to Kayin and to us the great
secret of the order of the world, that among His creations He placed
an entity designed to entrap man to do the wrong thing. If man sur-
mounts temptation, his accomplishment and reward are magnified,
and if not, Hashem has an additional reason to show His mercy.*

WHY COULDN'T KAYIN AND HEVEL GET ALONG?

> 4:8. And Kayin said to Hevel, and it was when
> they were in the field, Kayin rose against Hevel
> and killed him.

*Rashi: He entered into words of quarrel and contention with him
to find a pretext to kill him. There are aggadic midrashim about
this...*

Gur Arye: There are three versions of the argument [BR 22:7].
Some hold that Kayin took all the real estate in the world and
Hevel all the chattels. This one said the other was standing on
his land and that one said the first was wearing his clothes. Some
say they argued over the Holy Temple site, each claiming it as his
portion. Some say they both wanted the second triplet sister of
Hevel.[46]

Kayin and Hevel were two opposites, and as long as they
were able to remain separate without having to share anything
there was *shalom* [peace, harmony] between them. This concept
bears a similarity to the "*shalom*" between the angel Gavriel, who
is fire,[47] and the angel Michael, who is water [Num. R. 12:8]. But

---

46. Rashi, Sot. 9b: Kayin claimed her as firstborn [entitled to a double portion]
and Hevel claimed her for she was born with him [she was his womb mate].
47. Maharal, Netiv Hashalom 1, 1:215a: That is how it is in the world – each opposite receives from Hashem what the other does not, and that is *shalom*.
Fire receives from Hashem that which water does not...and Hashem makes
shalom between them...Even in the upper spheres *shalom* is needed for opposites to exist in the same world. Michael is appointed over the water and
Gavriel over the fire, and if it were not for *shalom*, each would cancel the other.
Gur Arye, Num. 20:29: Aharon pursued *shalom* between husband and wife by
making two switches, speaking to the husband about one specific matter and
the wife about another till he found common ground on which they could
agree and arrive at *shalom*. Chidushei Agadot on Shab. 25b, 1:8b: Shabbat light
makes *shalom* by separating things the way the pot makes peace between the
fire and the water. When it turns dark, it is called *erev* [mixture, evening], for

the brothers were opposite without a separation, for each entered the territory of the other. The land was fitting for Kayin but Hevel had to stand on it. Hevel had wool but Kayin had to clothe himself with it and invade his brother's domain. Therefore, there was no *shalom* and dispute came between them.

According to the opinion that they disputed the site of the Holy Temple, this site has the distinction of including the potential of both Kayin and Hevel. The proof of this is the permissibility of the mixture of wool and linen in the Holy Temple.[48] Here the brothers, opposites, had to share the same space, resulting in the dispute. Certainly it was fitting for the place at the center of the world [Tanchuma, Kedoshim 10], to be desired by both brothers.[49]

The opinion that they argued over the triplet relates to her association with Shabbat [4:2[3]], which is rest for all the days,[50] common shared time by Kayin and Hevel.

Each of the three opinions attributes the dispute to overlapping domains that required sharing by the brothers, who were opposites. The first opinion relates the dispute to the sharing of wealth, both property and movable objects. The second opinion relates to the sharing of ownership of the site of the Holy Temple, the main matter in the success of the *nefesh* [spirituality or soul

---

in the dark everything appears mixed, and when it turns light it is called *boker* [examination, morning], for things can be examined and differentiated. Now there can be *shalom* between things and nothing gets mixed up with anything else. Shabbat light clarifies the murky darkness, which drives away confusion and promotes peace.

48. Rashi, 'Ar. 3b: *Kilayim*: The priestly vestments contained the forbidden mixture of linen and wool, as it is written [Ex. 39:29]: "And the belt of woven linen…" and blue wool.

49. See Gevurot Hashem 9:52a and 71:325a, Derech Hachaim 5, 2:270b, Be'er Hagola 6:131b. Also see Gur Arye 28:17[23], Ket. 5a, and Gur Arye, Ex. 15:17.

50. Chidushei Agadot on Shab. 118a, 1:55b: Shabbat among the days is like the heart among the organs.

attached to the body].[51] In the third opinion they fought over a woman, which relates to body, for "His wife is like his body" [Ber. 24a].[52] In each opinion the conclusion is the same, and the brothers failed to share the common domain. The words of the sages are all true.

MDK: The three versions do not conflict with each other, and any or all may be correct. The common metaphysical lesson is that when opposites cannot share common ground, destruction ensues. The only remedy is separation, like the pot separating the water and the fire, or Divine intervention, as occurs between human male and female mates.

---

51. Gur Arye, Ex. 30:15: Sacrifices atone for souls. Rashi, Deut. 3:25: The Holy Temple is called Levanon [white] because it whitens the sins of Israel.
52. Derech Hachaim on 2:9, 89a divides man into three aspects – wealth, *nefesh*, and body. See also 2:5, 79b and introduction, p. 9 and Netiv Ha'avoda 3, 1:82b and Tiferet Yisrael 1, 8a.

SARCASM OR CONTRITION?

4:13. And Kayin said to Hashem, "My sin is too great to bear."

And Kayin said to Hashem, "Is my sin too great to bear?"

Rashi: This is read bitmia *[with wonderment, sarcasm] – You bear the higher realms and the lower realms, so is my iniquity impossible to bear?*

Gur Arye: Rashi, quoting midrash [BR 22:11] knows this because one could not interpret it as a confession for his sin,[53] for why say "impossible to bear" and declare that Hashem cannot forgive it? That would be self-prosecution.[54]

MDK: The Masoretic text has no punctuation marks, giving rise to a great dispute on this verse. Rashi closes this verse with a question mark, while Ramban does so with a period. According to Rashi, Kayin is challenging Hashem with sarcasm, true to his evil character. According to Ramban, Kayin is contrite, pleading for mercy. Both are "words of the Living God."

It has been said that Ramban disputes Rashi when he wants to set up a kabbalistic thought. In this case, the Zohar [Gen. 54b] states that Kayin's contrition resulted in Hashem cancelling half his punishment. This is congruent with Ramban's period but not with Rashi's question mark.

---

53. Ramban: The correct simple interpretation is that it is a confession.... Kayin said: My sin is great, and You have punished me exceedingly, but guard me that I should not be punished more than You decreed...The beasts will kill me.

54. Pachad Yitzchak disagrees in R.H. 21:8: By confession the sinner prosecutes himself, so that the heavenly prosecutor withdraws when they tell him someone has preceded him. This is the way of "If there is a deprecating matter in you, you be the one to say it first" [B.K. 92b].

DOUBLE ENTENDRE

> 4:26. Then it was begun [*huchal*] to call in the
> Name of Hashem.

Rashi: It means to call the names of men and the names of icons by the Name of the Holy One, blessed be He, to make of them idols and call them deities.

Gur Arye: There is a way to see this verse in a favorable sense – do we not invoke Hashem when we say "Blessed be Hashem" or "if Hashem wishes"? Avraham [21:33] "called in the Name of Hashem." How does Rashi know that "to call in the Name of Hashem" relates to idolatry? The answer is that since Kayin and Hevel had already called in Hashem's Name by their offerings [4:3 and 4:4], "begun to call" does not fit the context here. Additionally, the common word for begin is *hitchil* – why does the Torah use *huchal*? Although the simple translation of the latter is "begun," an additional meaning is "profaned." It is a major fundamental principle that the Torah often uses a play on words "language falling upon language" [double entendre] to reveal the interpretation of a word. Onkelos also renders it "profane." Similarly, the rabbis said [BR 23:7]: "In three places this expression is mentioned, and each refers to rebellion: our verse, 'and it was when man began to multiply' [6:8], and 'he began to be a powerful hunter' [10:8], all of them meaning "begin" with a connotation of "profane." Ibn Ezra explains the verse in a favorable sense but the spirit of the sages does not rest with this, because of the context of this chapter.

MDK: The context Gur Arye refers to is the theme of Genesis from the fall of Adam and Chava till the arrival of Avraham – that man has free will but will generally exercise it badly. Adam, Chava, Kayin, Hevel, Lemech, Noach, Cham, Kenaan, and Nimrod are all bad actors. The evil inclination overpowers them – Hashem has set the bar too high for them. Only Avraham can end the Age of Tohu and bring in the Age of Torah.

Gur Aye here introduces us to a fundamental principle of par-shanut [the mechanics of interpretation]. Whenever a word in the text has more than one meaning, the text must be learned using each meaning.

MAN CAN CORRUPT THE ANGELS

6:6. And Hashem was comforted that He had
made man on earth.

*Rashi: Hashem was consoled that He had made man a creature of
the lower realms, for had man been of the upper realms he would
have turned them to rebellion.*

Gur Arye: As Shlomo said, "There is no righteous one on earth
who will do good and not sin" [Eccl. 7:20], and man is intrinsi-
cally subject to sin.[55] Had man been of the upper realm, the angels
would have a "disordered behavior" [a term for sin as it applies
to angels who cannot sin] fitting them as well. If only individu-
als had sinned, the Torah would not have mentioned His "taking
comfort" here, but since the whole generation was evil, they could
have corrupted heaven. Note that though man was not created
in the upper realms, he was created of the upper realms partially
[Rashi 2:7], and the "upper" spiritual component of man, the
neshama [soul], is subject to sin. Others hold [BR 27:4] that sin
comes only by way of the body, and although "the evil soul desires
evil" [Prov. 21:10], this refers to the part of the soul [*nefesh*] that
is connected to the body.

*MDK: Maharal does not try to reconcile the opposite opinions of
our sages, of blessed memory. Elsewhere, he posits that sexual immorality is a sin of* guf, *bloodshed a sin of* nefesh, *and idolatry a
sin of* neshama.

---

55. 1:12[33], Derasha Leshabbat Hagadol 202a, and Derech Hachaim 3:9, 130a.

FOR EVERY THING THERE IS A SEASON

6:6. And He was pained in His heart.

Rashi: He mourned over the destruction of His handiwork, as in "The king was pained over his son" [Sam. 1 19:3]. In response to heretics who question the omniscience of Hashem here – if He knew He would later destroy them and mourn for them, why create them in the first place? – I bring the midrash [BR 27:4]: A non-believer asked Rabbi Yehoshua ben Karcha:

"Do you not admit that Hashem sees the future?"

"Yes."

"But it is written: 'He was pained in His heart.'"

"Did you ever have a son?"

"Yes."

"What did you do?"

"I rejoiced and made everyone rejoice."

"But did you not know his destiny is to die?"

"At a time of joy, there is joy, at a time of mourning, there is mourning."

"Such was the conduct of the Holy One, blessed be He. Even though it was revealed to Him that their destiny was sin and destruction, He did not refrain from creating them."

Gur Arye: There is a fundamental principle of the Torah here. The conduct of the world is by way of good, but some bad is mixed in. The good is the main thing and bad can be at its side. The good is what causes the world to exist.[56] Hashem seems to react to His own action, as in "Hashem will rejoice in His deeds" [Ps. 104:31] and here "He was pained."

There are two responses to Hashem's view of man's behavior, the permanent satisfaction resulting from when they are good

---

56. Derech Hachaim 1:2, 24a and Ramban 6:1: Evil depends on the continued existence of good.

and the fleeting dissatisfaction when they are evil. He created the world for the good but did not refrain from creating it on account of the bad. Nevertheless, when the bad came, He was pained

MDK: Rashi's parable means the response is matched to the circumstance. Even Hashem has, if it could be said, "a time to weep and a time to laugh" [Ecc. 3:4].

Noach

MAN GIVES BIRTH TO HIMSELF

6:9. These are the offspring of Noach – Noach was a righteous man, perfect in his generations; Noach walked with Hashem.

Rashi: This teaches you that the main toldot [*offspring, products*] *of the righteous are good deeds.*

Gur Arye: Deeds are the "fruit" man gives birth to.[1] By saying "main products," Rashi is alluding to the precedence of deeds over children. It appears to me that in the case of children, man is a partner with his wife and the Holy One, blessed be He, with the latter being the more important, for He contributes ten parts and each parent only five [Nid. 31a]. However, when a man creates a deed it is his alone. The main products of man are good deeds because children are not intrinsic to him while deeds are intrinsic to him. It is as if man gives birth to himself.

---

1. Sota, 46a: Why does the Torah say to bring a calf to the riverbed? Hashem says to bring something which has not borne fruit and break its neck in a place that makes no fruit and atone for one who did not allow his victim to bear fruit. What is fruit? The fulfillment of commandments. See Tiferet Yisrael 3:12a and Chidushei Agadot on Sot. 46a, 2:82b.

TWO KINDS OF DESTRUCTION

> 6:13. The end of all flesh has come before me…
> behold, I am about to destroy them from the
> earth.

Rashi: Wherever you find sexual immorality, epidemic disease comes to the world and kills good and bad.

Gur Arye: The angel of death is equated with epidemic disease.[2] The flow of the narrative is as follows: sexual immorality will bring pestilence/angel of death, so go hide yourself in the ark. The destroying angel has been given permission to kill all in his path, good and bad together, just as on Pesach night [Ex. 12:22], "you shall not go out of your door." But if the righteous one is not in the vicinity of the wicked one, the former will not be killed. Noach is in danger, but he can save himself and his family.

Notable is the use of *hashchata* [corruption, destruction] for both sexual immorality and pestilence/angel of death. *Hashchata* is total, destroying root and foundation, which means the righteous.[3] *Hashchata* is mentioned in connection with idolatry [Deut 4:16], but idolatry is different, for it is a sin directed against Hashem specifically,[4] and Hashem punishes for it Himself;[5] and unlike the pestilence/angel of death, He does differentiate between good and evil. Consider that sexual immorality is a sin of the body

---

2. B.K. 60b: When there is an epidemic in the city, do not walk in the middle of the road, for the angel of death walks in the middle of the road.

3. Prov. 10:25: The righteous one is the foundation of the world. Yom. 38b: The world continues even on account of a single righteous person. Hag. 12b: On what does the earth stand? On a single pillar, and Righteous is its name.

4. See Be'er Hagola 4:73a and Netzach Yisrael 3:18b.

5. Lev. 20:3: And I will turn My face to this man [the idolator king] and cut him off from the midst of his people. Rashi, ad. loc.: I will put aside all My business and deal with him.

of man[6] which provokes bodily destruction.[7, 8] Idolatry is a sin of the *nefesh* [soul, spirit], the province of Hashem Himself. The punishment it provokes is specific to the wicked *nefesh*.

MDK: This is one of the answers to the theologic problem of why bad things happen to good people – Hashem can unleash destructive forces that do not discriminate among their victims.

---

6. See Netiv Hashalom 6, 2:75b. Chidushei Agadot on A.Z. 5b, 4:32a: *Chamor* [donkey, physicality] is the inclination to sexual immorality, an act of physicality, hinted at [Sot. 15b] in the sacrifice of the suspected wife – since she allegedly acted like a donkey, her sacrifice is barley – donkey food.
7. Ibid: Idolatry is a spiritual force that pertains to the soul, not the body.
8. Eccl. 9:2: A single outcome occurs to righteous and wicked. Rashi, ad. loc.: This world has one outcome for all – death. The righteous know this but they still choose the right way, for they know they have a better fate than the wicked in the World to Come.

THE EVIL INCLINATION ATTACKS
AFTER A GOAL IS ACHIEVED

8:21. The inclination of man's heart is evil from his youth [*min'urav*].

Rashi: Min'urav is written without a vav, *as if it were read* min'arav, *which means from the time he stirs. From the time he stirs to go out of his mother's womb the urge to do evil is put in him.*

Gur Arye: Urges develop in people who have attained some stage of completion or *shelemut*. If one is in motion toward a goal, his effort is directed to the achievement of that goal; he looks neither to the left nor to the right. How then does sin come into being? A person perceives a lacking in himself and has an urge to remedy it. This urge may be for something forbidden. This perception of lacking that leads to the sin occurs only after he has advanced himself to some plateau and achieved some goal, but not while in motion toward that goal. Consider the fetus, incomplete, undeveloped, striving to ready himself for emergence from the womb.[9] The evil inclination will not start up with him till he achieves some level of when he is ready and stirs to leave the womb. The principle extends to levels of *shelemut* as the rabbis hinted [Suk.

---

9. Derech Hachaim 2:2 on, "The exertion of Torah with *derech eretz* makes sin forgotten," 71b: Sin occurs when there is sitting as opposed to hard work. A worker is by definition incomplete, a work in progress, for the goal of his work is to attain *shelemut*. While he works and moves, defects and failings are not noted. But when he completes his work and reaches a level of *shelemut*, he is drawn to his failings, for every completed work has something lacking. The *Gemara* states [Sanh. 91b]: When is the evil inclination placed in man? From the moment he emerges from his mother – till then he is in motion and urges do not cleave to him.

52a]: He who is greater than his peers, presumably with a greater degree of *shelemut*, has greater urges than they do.[10]

The *Gemara* [Yom. 82b] discusses a case of a pregnant woman with an irresistible urge to eat on Yom Kippur, her fetus having smelled a certain food. Rabbi Chanina whispered in her ear to the fetus that that day was Yom Kippur, but the lust of the fetus continued. Whereupon Rabbi Chanina recited the verse [Ps. 58:4], "The wicked are estranged in the womb (from the ways of the Torah – see Rashi there)." The fetus grew up to be Shabtai the fruit-storer, whose manipulative practices drove up the price of fruit and made it unavailable to the people. If the evil inclination does not enter till birth, how was this fetus "estranged" and "evil"? The answer is that evil may arise after birth under the "nurturing" influence of the evil inclination or, in the exceptional case, evil may be naturally inherent in his being. The prophet says of the righteous [Jer. 1:5], "Before you emerged from the womb I knew you" – this does not mean the fetus acted with intent and will, for the good inclination does not enter the person till age thirteen [Eccl. R. 4:13].

Just what is inclination? It is the thought that yearns for good or bad. The fetus, possessing no inclination as we have defined it, acts in accord with its nature. This explains what happened in Rivka's womb, where Esav stirred when she passed a house of idolatry [25:22].[11]

MDK: Gur Arye seems to imply that having granted man free will, Hashem tests him by way of his nature and his nurture. Sometimes, and this may be rare, He creates in him an evil nature – "the evil soul craves evil" [Prov. 21:10] – to wit, Kayin, Esav, Shabtai the

---

10. See Netzach Yisrael 2:13a. Also Tiferet Yisrael 48:148: Only after Israel accepted the Torah did Satan start up with them to sin.
11. 25:22[25]: What Esav did was not on account of his inclination, but rather a manifestation of his returning to his type and his nature…See 6:6[11]{41}.

fruit-storer. Generally, He provides a Satan/evil inclination to nurture temptation [Gen.4:7]. The result is "there is no righteous man on earth who does only good and does not sin" [Eccl. 7:20].

THE SECRET OF NOACH'S THREE SONS

9:23. And Shem and Yefet took [this verb is in the singular] the garment…

Rashi: "Took" is singular even though there are two subjects, to teach that Shem took the initiative and predominated in the meritorious act. Therefore his offspring merited the commandment to wear tzitzit [fringes], while the offspring of Yefet merited burial, as it says [Ezek. 39:11], "I will give Gog a place of burial there." And Cham, who shamed his father, his offspring were exiled [Isa. 20:4], "tattered, barefoot, and with buttocks bared."

Gur Arye: A fundamental midrashic principle is that [BR 36:6] children are drawn to their progenitors. The verse tells us Cham "uncovered nakedness" and shamed the body by shaming his father [9:22], and his offspring followed in his footsteps in an egregious fashion. Shem and Yafet conducted themselves honorably and their offspring continued with honor.[12] The children of Shem merited the *mitzva* of *tzitzit*, for the Honor of Hashem enwraps them and is upon them. Shem was more honored than Yefet because he aggressively pursued the meritorious deed – both his body and his soul were honored. Yefet's participation in the act of covering their father was done without his soul's intent but with his body alone, so the body that did the good deed was honored.[13]

This midrash contains a remarkable secret. Consider the three sons and their levels[14] – Shem, the honored and choicest,

---

12. Chidushei Agadot on Sanh. 70a, 3:169b: The whole world came out of the sons of Noach…Cham specialized in sexual immorality, therefore out of him came the likes of Kenaan and Mitzraim, all of them licentious. Shem and Yefet dealt with the concealment of nakedness and were rewarded.

13. Netiv Hazerizut 2, 2:188a: Endeavor and enthusiasm have their roots in man's soul, while laziness is a result of the body. Enthusiasm in the fulfillment of a commandment makes it completely Godly.

14. See Chidushei Agadot on Ned. 32b, 2:12a.

Yefet the elder,[15] and Cham the younger. Yefet lacked enthusiasm for his action came from the body whose action lacks enthusiasm,[16] thus he merited that the body be buried. His name Yefet [beauty] is fitting because beauty pertains only to the body. Cham is the force of the soul and he bears the power of the vital force – the natural heat [*chom*] in the heart of man, thus his name is Cham. But *shem* [name][17] is the main principle,[18] the essence of the *tzura* [spiritual character] of man, thus his name is Shem. Now you can understand the secret of the three sons – that each represents a portion of man. Yefet corresponds to body, which accounts for his laziness. Cham corresponds to *nefesh hachiuni* [living soul, vital force, shared with all living things, bearer of the spiritual soul],[19] who is cursed to be a slave [9:25] and whose descendant,

---

15. 10:21: "The brother of the elder Yefet." Gevurot Hashem, introduction 3:20a: In the future, Gog and Magog will come to be exalted…on account of their being from the seed of Yefet, who is referred to as *gadol* [greater, elder]. Understand that the second brother is called Shem, for he is the portion of Hashem out of whom will come Israel, yet Yefet is even more *gadol*, worthy of exultation.

16. Gevurot Hashem 15:74b: Israel does not have the coarseness of physicality, so that the force of their nature acts more quickly, and they gave birth speedily like the beasts of the field. Preface to Pachad Yitzchak: Lightwaves move faster than other worldly forces. This results from the basic principle that light is the purest and most widespread force in the natural world. The saintly Luzzato has written [Mesilat Yesharim, Ch. 6] that what impedes the speed of movement is the coarseness that is the leadenness of physicality.

17. 6:4[9]<35> and 14:14[26] and Or Chadash 110a: The name in every instance teaches about identity. Adam was so named to teach us of his creation from *adama* [earth]. Chidushei Agadot on R.H. 16b, 1:108a: When a person's name is changed, his decree is torn up because a person's name points to his essence and a change of name is a change of essence. The name is most important, as the *Gemara* says [Ber. 7b]: The name causes things to happen. See Chidushei Agadot on Git. 2:99a on Kamtza, Tiferet Yisrael 21:67a on Moshe, Derech Hachaim on 5:19, 266b on Avraham and Bilam.

18. 2:15[32]<93> and 4:8[10]<71> develop the idea that the essense of man is his *tzura* [spiritual character].

19. Derech Hachaim on 2:8, 86a: The living soul is to be distinguished from the speaking soul which is not shared in common with all other living things.

Eliezer, is told "stay here with the donkey" [22:5], on which the rabbis commented, "A nation comparable to a donkey" [Yev. 62a].[20] Although Yefet is body, it is appropriate for him.[21] The difference is that Yefet lacks *tzura* [spirituality] while Cham has it in an accursed, corrupted form.[22]

You will find that these three sons correspond to the three sons of Adam.[23] Both sets of sons included the whole world. Yefet corresponds to Hevel, as King Shlomo says in A Woman of Valor, "grace is false and beauty (*yofi*) is *hevel* [vain]" [Prov. 31:30] and both relate to the body.[24] Cham was cursed like Kayin was cursed [4:11]. And Shem, the most important as was explained, corresponds to Shet who was the foundation and the most important, called Shet for from him the whole world was established [*hushtat*] [Num. R. 14:12].

MDK: All this is hinted at by the singular "took" in our verse.

Additionally, man has the separate *sechel* [spirituality, intelligence] which has no connection to the body.

20. See Derech Hachaim on 2:9, 91a and Chidushei Agadot on b.b. 58a, 3:82a and 14:14[26]. Gevurot Hashem 4:31a: The Kena'anim are the deficient, cursed form worthy of servitude. Tiferet Yisrael 37:108a: Servitude is physical and subordinate to the spiritual, which is free. The subordinate slave is physical the same way a donkey is physical.

21. See Gur Arye, Ex. 2:14.

22. Be'er Hagola 5:103a.

23. 4:3[5,6,10]

24. 4:3[6]<48>.

NIMROD

10:8. And Cush begat Nimrod – he began [*hechel*]
to be a mighty man on earth.

*Rashi: He was mighty in causing the whole world to rebel against
the Holy One, blessed be He, through the scheme of the generation
of dispersion discussed later in this section.*

Gur Arye: Otherwise it could have said "he was the first mighty
man." But he began something here – the worldwide rebellion
against Hashem, and *hechel* connotes "profaned" as well as "began" as discussed earlier in the section called *Double Entendre*.[25]
But there were idolaters before[26] – why say Nimrod began it? Because the verse goes on to say he was "mighty at trapping," which
means that he was the first to succeed in the entrapment of people's minds [Rashi 10:9].

    This midrashic explanation [BR 23:7] is inconsistent with the
tendency in scripture not to conceal misdeeds of sinners.[27] Why
speak so elliptically of Nimrod's sin? The answer is that idolatry was not a revealed matter in their day, just as the worship of
Hashem was not known. Neither is mentioned in the Torah till
much later.

    The simple interpretation is, as Onkelos renders, he was a
strong king.[28] But strength [*gevura*] applies only to Hashem, as
we say in the morning prayer, "Are not all mighty men like nothing before You?" He began to be mighty before Hashem when he

---

25. See 4:26[32].
26. Ramban here: Began must mean began after the flood, for they began in the
    days of Enosh, when as Rashi [4:26] said they began to call people and icons
    in Hashem's name. Also see 4:20[24].
27. See Num. R. 21:3 and 6:9[17]<101>.
28. Rashi, Pes. 94b: Nimrod was King of Bavel.

should have shown humility and submission,[29] which hints that his strength was the strength of rebellion and idolatry. "Mighty at trapping" connotes plotting and trickery, not going on the simple straight path like other trappers. "Before Hashem" connotes plotting and trickery in Godly matters to the point of causing the people to rebel against Hashem. Likewise Esav was [25:27] "a man who knew of trapping" as opposed to Yaakov, the simple, "pure man." Nimrod was the first king, and otherwise unspecified earthly kings oppose the Kingdom of Heaven, which is why Hashem did not wish for Israel to appoint a king over themselves.[30] True are the words of the sages.[31]

MDK: Here Gur Arye defends Rashi's interpretation against Ramban and against the commentators who accept the translation of Onkelos.

---

29. Kings I 21:29, Kings II 22:19, and Chron. II 35:23 are examples of "before" implying submission.
30. Sanh. 20b: Hashem allowed Israel to appoint a king [Deut. 17:14–15] only to deter resentment. Rabbenu Bechaye, Deut. 17:14: It is not the will of the Holy One, blessed be He, that there be any King of Israel but He, for He is the King that walks in the midst of their encampment…They need no other king, for the chosen people over whom the Master of all is King – what will they do with a king of flesh and blood?
31. Er. 53a.

THE TOWER IN THE VALLEY

> 11:1. And it was that all the world was one language and unified words.

Rashi: *The one language was the holy language [Hebrew].*

Gur Arye: The world was created with the holy language, as we established from that which is written [2:23] "for from man was she taken." The midrash notes [BR 18:4] that naming her *isha* [woman] for this reason only makes sense if the names of man and woman are linguistically related. Among ancient languages this only occurs in Hebrew. It follows that Hashem spoke the holy language to create the world[32] and that would be the one language the world spoke at that time.

Rashi: *"Unified words" means they came with one plan of action and they said, "Hashem has no right to select the upper realms for Himself. We will go up to the firmament and wage war with Him." Alternatively,* devarim achadim *could mean matters of Oneness, words against the Singular One of the world. Alternatively they said, "Every 1656 years the firmament collapses. Come let us make buttresses for it."*

Gur Arye: In Rashi's first explanation they built the tower to penetrate the upper realms so as to enter there. The war would be an effort to cancel Hashem's decrees, assuming the source of His authority to be His Oneness in the upper realms. They said that man is in the lower realms, which makes him very deficient. The tower with its top in the heavens would allow the residents of the lower realms to go up and live there too…Their being in the upper realms would cancel the power that derives from Him being over them. In the lower realms, man is one, capable of waging war

---

32. Ab. 5:1: With ten sayings the world was created.

with the One of the upper realms, for it is impossible that there be two "ones" in the same place.[33]

It is surprising that [Sanh. 109a] Rabbi Shela [of Babylonia] taught that the generation of dispersion said, "Let us go up to the firmament and smite it with battering rams, and its water will flow." Upon hearing this, the rabbis of the West [the Land of Israel] laughed and retorted, "If so, why build it in a valley? Why not a mountaintop?"

What were the two sides in this dispute? Rabbi Shela held they wished only to make a representation or model of puncturing the firmament, such that building the tower in a valley would suffice. The rabbis of the West mocked this, for if they wished to ascend it would have been far easier from a mountaintop. Rashi, quoting the midrash [BR 38:6], also assumes their purpose was ascent and is left with the mocking question of the rabbis of the West – why not build it on a mountaintop? The answer is that Rashi's midrash does not require actual entry into the upper realms, just a symbol of "reaching the sky," thus "waging war" by challenging Hashem. In their eyes, by building "it's top in heaven" [11:4] they would violate the principle of "The heaven is the heaven of Hashem, and the earth He gave to the sons of man" [Ps. 115:16]. The tower was to be considered separate from the earth, a challenge to the authority of Hashem – in short, war.

Rashi's first explanation of "unified words" is [talk of] war, the second, [talk of] idolatry, and the third, [talk of] a civil engineering project. The generation of dispersion postulated that since the flood occurred 1656 years after creation it was due to occur again. The number is derived by adding the ages of the fathers, from Adam to Noach, at which their sons were born [Gen. 5] to the 100 years of Noach's oldest son at the time of the flood. If floods resulted periodically from the earth's orbit, the tower could interfere with the orbit or buttress the firmament and prevent the flood.

---

33. Chidushei Agadot on Sanh. 109a, 3:260b.

WHEN THE LIGHT COMES, THE
DARKNESS DISAPPEARS

11:32. And Terach died in Charan.

Rashi: This happened more than sixty years after his son Avraham left Charan and came to the land of Kenaan...Why did the Torah first mention the death of Terach, then the departure of Avraham? In order not to call to the attention of all that Avraham did not fulfill honoring his father, leaving the old man and going on his way, so the Torah pronounced [Terach] dead. For the wicked are called dead in their lifetime and the righteous are called alive even after they die.

Gur Arye: What does Rashi mean by "calling to the attention of all"? Was the Torah not given to scholars who can calculate for themselves that Terach was alive long after Avraham left? This is what the midrash [BR 39:7] actually said: "Rabbi Yitzchak said: If one calculates, Terach lived another sixty-five years, but it must be interpreted that the wicked are called dead in their lifetime. Avraham feared profaning the Name of Heaven on account of his abandoning his father. Hashem told him, 'Go, I absolve you of the honoring of your parents, but I absolve no one else. Furthermore, in My Book his death will appear before your departure so it will not seem as if you left him.'"

A deeper matter is hinted at here. Honoring one's father applies if there is a relationship between the father and the son. Avraham was not really related to his father – Avraham was a new beginning, a new creation.[34] The sages said [A.Z. 9a] that the world consists of six thousand years – two thousand years of *tohu*, two thousand years of Torah, and two thousand years of redemption. From creation till Avram was fifty-two years old, everything was

---

34. Gevurot Hashem 5:32b. See Derech Hachaim 5:2, 209b and 5:4, 224b and Gur Arye, 21:33[28].

tohu [confusion, amazement] for there was no Torah (according to the chronology established by the rabbis based on the verses in the Torah, Avram was born in the year 1948).

The reason Hashem absolved him of honoring his father[35] was that Avraham was unique among men in that he had no connection or relationship to his father, like the light has no connection to the darkness. Avraham was the light and the earlier generations were *tohu* and darkness. All the generations from Noach to Avraham existed only to produce Avraham,[36] who is the main factor in the building of the world. He is a different creation, unrelated to his father and the previous generations of *tohu*. When the light comes, the darkness disappears, such that for Avraham's story to begin it is proper to speak of the exit of Terach.

It is most remarkable that the wicked are called dead during their life [BR 39:7] for life is like "living water" [Num. 19:17] which flows without stop.[37] Since their life ceases with their death, it cannot be called lifetime, for by definition life is unstoppable. Since they die, they are called dead during their life. Conversely, the righteous are called living even in death [Ber. 18a][38] because they are set to return to life at the resurrection. Consider that Hashem is the "source of life" [Ps. 36:10]. Life is called "living water" [Num. 19:17] when it flows from the One Source – the life of the wicked does not flow from there. A pit may hold much water but has no source and is not called *chaim* [alive, flowing]. Conversely, the life of the righteous even after death is called life, like a spring flow-

---

35. Gevurot Hashem 5:34b.
36. See Rashi 37:1 and Derech Hachaim 5:3,219b.
37. See Derech Hachaim 6:8,307b and Netiv Hatorah 4:1,20b and 29:11[7].
38. Chidushei Agadot on R.H. 16b, 1:109b: The righteous cleave to the source of life after they die and, even if they are not alive in actuality, they have some minimal attachment to life, as it is written [Deut. 4:4], "And you who cleave to Hashem your God are all alive today." Since the Source of Life does not cease, you will live forever just as you live today. In the case of the wicked, he is cut off and completely removed from life. See also 18:19[48], 30:1[3], and Ex. 4:19[12].

ing from a distant source which becomes obstructed. The water may temporarily be held up, but as the source continues to flow, eventually the spring will flow again. Death is such a temporary "physical" barrier – nature makes a barrier between the righteous person and his source until Hashem supersedes nature and the dead will come alive.

Avraham attains his exalted status with his departure to Kenaan.[39] His light shines and the darkness disappears. Thus this event is related to the "death" of his father.

Ramban asks, didn't Terach repent? Rashi explains the verse [15:15], "And you will come to your fathers in peace," that he repented. If so, he was not wicked! The answer is his atonement came only with his death. During his life he was called dead, but his actual death atoned for him,[40] for "all death atones" [Sifri, Shelach 15:31].[41] A better way to formulate Terach's atonement is that although he repented, his forgiveness was *talui* [conditional, dependent, hanging] until his death completed his atonement. Thus during his lifetime he was considered dead.

MDK: The mention of Terach's death demarcates the epoch of tohu from the epoch of Torah. Our attention is called to it by virtue of its chronologic displacement. Gur Arye takes this opportunity to introduce the secret of the meaning of life – the attachment to Hashem through the Wellspring of Living Waters.

---

39. Derech Hachaim on 5:9, 247a: The exalted status of the patriarchs derived specifically from the Land of Israel. Otherwise, they would not have the highest level of *kedusha* [holiness, separateness, dedication]. The Land raised them, and from this you know that the patriarchs belong to the Land and the Land to the patriarchs. See Zohar 1:79b.
40. Gevurot Hashem 5:35 and Yom. 66a.
41. See 21:17[20]. A third formulation is found in Gevurot Hashem 5:34: Some say that Hashem only accepted Terach's repentance on account of his son Avraham.

Addenda

WHAT DID THEY KNOW AND WHEN DID THEY KNOW IT?

> 3:7. The eyes of the two of them were opened and they realized they were naked.

Rashi: The verse speaks of wisdom rather than the sense of sight, for even a blind man knows when he is naked.

Gur Arye: We have evidence that Adam and Chava had knowledge before they ate from the Tree of Knowledge. Adam named the creatures [2:20] and had *sechel* [intelligence, spirituality] and a grasp of reality,[1] but it seems he only had a grasp of the positive aspect of things, like the Creator, and existence. But to grasp the negative aspect of things, such as that they were naked – that they did not know before now. Thus the rabbis said [BR 19:5] "the Tree of Knowledge increases knowledge" – this is the wisdom referred to. To grasp that there is shame in standing naked, this they acquired from eating of the Tree of Knowledge. So writes Rambam in his *Guide to the Perplexed* [1:2].

---

1. Mizrachi: It does not mean that Hashem did not give them wisdom from the beginning and now gave it, as Rashi says on "they were not embarrassed" [2:25]: He gave Adam the knowledge to name the animals and birds.

MDK: Rashi disabuses us of the notion of the literal meaning of the verse. Gur Arye explores what they did and did not know and what the effect of ingesting the fruit of the Tree of Knowledge was.

> 3:22. Behold, man became as one of us, to know
> good and evil…

Rashi: He is unique in the lower spheres as I am unique in the upper spheres. What is his uniqueness? Knowing good and evil, unlike all other creatures in the lower spheres.

Gur Arye: Rashi previously informed us [2:25] that when the verse remarks that Adam and Chava before the sin "were not ashamed," it meant that they did not distinguish between good and evil, and therefore did not know the ways of *tzeniut* [modesty]. Since Hashem knows all, He certainly knows the ways of *tzeniut*, that it is indecent to stand naked.[2] But man did not have a grasp of this until he incorporated the evil inclination.[3] Lacking that, he was far away from grasping the concept of *tzeniut*. Thus the *tzeniut* definition of "knowing good and evil" is symmetrical – Adam in the lower spheres has become as Hashem in the upper.

Mizrachi posits another interpretation that "knowing good and evil" is *sechel* and awareness. Since angels have *sechel*, Mizrachi was troubled by the lack of symmetry, assuming man's uniqueness is *sechel* and God's uniqueness is something other than *sechel* – i.e., Godliness. The answer is that the symmetry lies in the uniqueness itself. Likewise, the rabbis said, when Avraham

---

2. Yeb. 63b: There is nothing more abominable and despicable before the Omnipresent than he who walks naked in the marketplace.

3. See 3:7[11]{17} and Derech Hachaim on 4:22, 206a: The additional *sechel* that Adam acquired was a detriment to him, for when man is *tamim* [pure, perfect, simple] he is drawn to Hashem…then he lives forever. *Tamim* refers to not having additional wisdom, for guile and scheming are beyond the bounds of *tamim*. Man, before he sinned, cleaved to Him, and his purpose was He and His utter Goodness, such that he knew only good…The snake told him that by eating from the Tree of Knowledge he would obtain additional knowledge, that of good and evil.

was thrown into the furnace, Gavriel asked the Holy One, blessed be He, if he could go down and save him, and was answered, "I am unique in my world and he is unique in his. It is nicer that a Unique One save a unique one." This does not mean equality in Mastery and Godliness, only that Hashem is unique in Godliness in His realm and Avraham unique in his, in that he alone entered under the wings of the Divine Presence [BR 42:3].[4] Uniqueness could also be explained in terms of wisdom – though the angels have wisdom and awareness, they bow to the wisdom and awareness of the Omniscient, parallel to the lower creatures bowing to the wisdom and awareness of man.

MDK: As this selection requires a great deal of mental energy, it belongs in the Addenda.

---

4. Derech Hachaim on 6:10, 318a: Avraham was the first righteous man, making him unique, as it is explicitly written [Isa. 51:2] "look at Avraham your father...for I called him unique." The one who initiates something is alone and unique.

Book III: Patriarchs And Matriarchs

Lech Lecha

THE BLESSING OF THE FATHERS

12:2. And I will make you a great nation, and I
will bless you, and I will make your name great,
and you will be a blessing.

*Rashi: [Another interpretation:] "I will make you a great nation" re-
fers to that which the Jewish People say in the* Amida *prayer "God
of Avraham," "and I will bless you" refers to "God of Yitzchak," "and
I will make your name great" refers to "God of Yaakov." One would
think the concluding blessing should include all three, but "and
you will be a blessing" comes to teach that they will conclude with
"Blessed are You, Hashem, shield of Avraham." With you they will
conclude the blessing, not the others.*

Gur Arye: Since all three are patriarchs, what is wrong with concluding with all three? It is because the formula for a long blessing [Ber. 49a] is to conclude with not more than one. Why should
the one be Avraham? Because the children are considered to be
within the potential of the father and not vice versa,[1] their concluding blessing is included in his.

    As discussed in Derech Hachaim [29b], the notion that
Yitzchak and Yaakov are included in Avraham applies to their attributes as well. The Mishna states [Ab. 1:2], "The world stands

---

1.   See Gevurot Hashem 9:58b and Derech Hachaim 6:10, 318a.

on three pillars – on Torah, on *avoda* [service to Hashem], and on *gemilut chasadim* [acts of kindness]." Avraham represented one pillar – Kindness, and he merited that Yitzchak, who represented the second pillar – Service – should come out of him. From Yitzchak and his pillar came out Yaakov representing the third pillar – Torah.

MDK: Note that kindness includes and subsumes and gives rise to service of Hashem, which includes, subsumes, and gives rise to Torah. This unidirectional inclusion principle applies not just to the patriarchs and their attributes but to the names of Hashem and His attributes as well. Thus, El Shadai, Whose attribute is Good, includes and subsumes YKVK, Whose attribute is Mercy, which in turn includes and subsumes Elokim, Whose attribute is Judgment. This is fully explained in Gur Arye's discussion of Avraham's plea for Sedom [18:23], which should be read in conjunction with this selection.

THE GENTILITY OF AVRAHAM

12:8: And he pitched his/her [written as hers, pronounced as his] tent.

Rashi: It is written as her tent. First he pitched his wife's tent and then his own.

Gur Arye: One would not say the opposite, that he pitched his own first. The reason is that when they differ, the written version takes precedence over the pronounced version.[2] And why did he pitch hers first? It is because a man must honor his wife more than himself [Hul. 84b].

MDK: There is an oral and a written version of the Masoretic Text, and they are not always congruent. Here, the written form is ohala *[her tent], but by our tradition from Sinai, it is pronounced* oholo *[his tent]. Such incongruencies are always subject to midrashic interpretation.*

---

2. Tosafot, Hag. 2a disagrees with the principle of the precedence of the written version. But even they would agree here that he pitched her tent first like the written version, for had he pitched his tent first, why does the Torah bother to allude to her tent at all? It must mean her tent comes first, to emphasize that a man must honor his wife more than himself. [Gur Arye, ad. loc.]

MIRACLES SHOULD BE MADE TO APPEAR NATURAL

14:14. And he armed his 318 acolytes, and gave chase as far as Dan.

Rashi: Acolytes refers to Eliezer, whose numerical equivalent in gematria is 318.

Gur Arye: Rabbenu Bechaye takes issue with this midrash [BR 43:2] brought by Rashi – what lesson can we learn from this *gematria?* I say the words of the rabbis, of blessed memory, are true, and the correspondence of the number of acolytes with Eliezer's name is no coincidence.

Avraham's pursuit and conquest of the kings was due to his exalted status.[3] The four kings were external forces coming from four sides to oppose Avraham and his message, monotheism and ethics. He was the basis and root of civilization, unique and singular. In opposition were the four sides or extremities, deviant aspects of reality, represented by the four kings.[4]

Avraham had a servant Eliezer who fittingly had an exalted status in servitude to match his master's uniqueness.[5] These two, without the help of another person, were capable of defeating the enemy. However, they did not want something natural to appear miraculous, and also the enemy would take strength from the small number opposing him.[6] A miracle can be strengthened

---

3. See Gevurot Hashem 5:37b and 10:60a.
4. Gevurot Hashem 10:60a.
5. Chidushei Agadot, B.B. 58a, 3:82a: Avraham's *gematria* is 248 corresponding to the number of man's organs [Tanchuma, Korach 12] concerning which the rabbis said [Ned. 32b] that Hashem gave him control over all his 248 parts. Such a person had serving him a man of giant stature and status. These two greats complimented each other and attested to one another's greatness.
6. Chidushei Agadot, Ned. 32b, 2:11a.

through natural means.[7] So he took his acolytes, but he took the exact number as Eliezer's *gematria*. He did not need them, but he did not want the victory to appear as a naked miracle, and he wanted the meaning and essence of Eliezer,[8] i.e., "my God helps," to be hidden in his force of acolytes.

MDK: Avraham, who brought to the world a knowledge of the King of kings, is opposed and attacked by the armies of four temporal kings from the four ends of the world. Their leader is Nimrod [Kedorla'omer], who has lost a series of confrontations with Avraham. In the midrash, the latter successfully disputes Nimrod's claim to be god, opposes the building of the doomed Tower of Bavel, and survives Nimrod's death penalty in the fiery furnace. This is the showdown, and Avraham wins hands down.

---

7.   Josh. 8:1–2: Behold I have given you the King of Ai. Make an ambush around the back of the city. Ramban 6:19: The size of the ark diminishes the magnitude of the miracle, for that is the way of miracles in the Torah and the Prophets, that they be done within the apparent capability of man, and the rest will be by the hand of heaven. See Rashi, Ex. 39:32 and Gur Arye, Ex. 25:31.
8.   Or Chadash 110a: The name always teaches about identity. The name Adam teaches us his identity, that he was created from *adama* [earth]. See 6:4[9].

LOOKING DOWN ON THE STARS

> 15:5. And He took him outside and He said, "Look [habet] toward the heaven and count the stars, if you are able to count them," and He said to him, "Thus will be your progeny."

Rashi: [Alternatively,] He took him outside the space of the universe, raising him above the stars. Habata [looking out] carries the connotation of from above to below.

Gur Arye: Perhaps to give Avraham the fullest perspective of the stars, Hashem takes him outside the universe. This interpretation hinges on the verb *habet*. Rashi defines *habata* as gazing downward, and the only way to see stars from above is from outside the space of the universe.

This assumption from the midrash [BR 48:12] is attacked by Mizrachi. *Habata* in the Torah is not always downward, as in [Ex. 33:8], "They looked behind Moshe"; [Ps. 142:5], "look to the right and see"; [19:26], "his wife looked behind him"; and [Num. 21:9], "he would look up at the copper snake." In all these examples, *habata* is other than downward. What Rashi really means is *habata* only applies if the object can theoretically be seen from above. The objects of Mizrachi's citations all could be seen from above if the viewer were, say, on a high hill. If they could be seen behind, to the right, or above, but also from above downward, this qualifies as *habata* by Rashi's definition. Not so the stars. To look down upon the stars one would have to be situated outside the space of the universe.

MDK: Gur Arye defends Rashi with a twist in the meaning of habata *that allows for the correctness of all the citations.*

THE PERFECTION OF AVRAHAM

17:1. Walk before Me and be perfect.

Rashi: …Alternatively, "be perfect" means at present you are defi-cient in five body parts – two eyes, two ears, and the male phallus. I will add a letter to your name and the numerical value of your name will be 248, the number of all your body parts.

Gur Arye: Sometimes, a person unintentionally sees something forbidden or hears an evil word unintentionally.[9] Before he un-derwent *mila* [ritual circumcision], Avraham was unique in that he was able to take care not to sin with all his body parts but five. By adding a *heh*, numerically equivalent to five, Hashem imparted to Avraham at the time of his *mila* kingship over all his organs. The defect the loathsome foreskin[10] confers to the phallus is re-moved, and even the eyes and ears are not used except for the per-formance of meritorious deeds. Initially, when he saw something bad, he had to conquer his evil inclination not to be drawn after it. Initially he had rulership [*memshala*], implying a lack of consent of the governed. For example, he could avert his gaze after the eye had transmitted an improper image. Now, after the *mila*,[11] he has kingship [*melucha*], implying consent of the governed,[12] such that the eye itself sees only that which is proper in Hashem's service. Now he does not need to conquer his inclination, for his entire inclination is within his domain. This is what the prophet means [Neh. 9:7–8] by "You are Hashem *Elokim* who chose Avram, and took him out of Ur Kasdim and made his name Avraham, and

9. Tanchuma, Toldot 12: Hashem created three things within man's domain – the hands, the feet, and the tongue, and three things outside his domain – the eyes, the ears, and the nose; man sees, hears, and smells automatically, with-out intent.
10. Rashi, Ned. 31a: As long as you have a foreskin you are defective before Me.
11. See Derech Hachaim 5:3, 220b and Netiv Ha'emuna 2, 1:201a.
12. Ibn Ezra 37:8. See Chidushei Agadot on Ned. 32b.

found his heart [*levavo*][13] faithful before You." His evil inclination had converted to good.

MDK: The midrash picks up on the numerology of the name change to propose a mechanism by which the mila *and the name change perfected Avraham – the conquest and enlistment of the evil inclination in the cause of goodness.*

Mila as a symbol of rulership might be considered a reason for Avraham being asked to hurt himself at the anatomic site of pleasure, to prove his mastery over it.

---

13. Ber. 54a: "With all your heart" [levavcha, spelled with two letters *bet*] means with both inclinations, the good and the evil [Rashi, Deut. 6:2].

TO FORSAKE THE LAND OF ISRAEL
IS TO FORSAKE HASHEM

17:8. And I will give you and your children after you the land where you live, all the Land of Kenaan, for a holding forever, and I will be their God.

Rashi: There I will be a God for them, but if one of them lives outside the Land it will be as if I will not be their God.

Gur Arye: Rashi means he will have no God to help and support him for that is what Hashem does.[14] For the Land of Israel is the land Hashem cares for, and His eyes are upon it from the beginning of the year till the end of the year [Deut. 11:12]. The other lands He apportioned to the angels,[15] and if one lives outside

---

14. Chron. II 32:8: Hashem, our God, is with us to help us.
15. Tanchuma, Re'e 8, Ramban, Deut. 7:6, and Lev. 18:25: Hashem, the Honored One, created all and placed the power over the lower spheres in the upper spheres. He gave each nation in its land a known star or planet, as is known to the astrologers, and over them *malachim* [angels, agents] to be rulers over them…But the Land of Israel, the center of the settlement of the world, is the specific inheritance over which He placed no angel, officer, marshal, or ruler, but transferred it to His people, the seed of His beloved. This is what is meant by "You will be more precious than all the nations, for the earth is Mine" [Ex.19:5]. He separated us from the nations and gave us the Land in order that He be a God to us. "There is no strange god with Him" [Deut. 32:12] means [Sifre, Ha'azinu 315] there will be no authority of one of the heavenly officers of the nations over you. The rabbis said [Ket. 110b], He who lives outside the Land is compared to one who has no God, as it says [Deut. 25:38], "to give you the Land of Kenaan to be a God to you," and as David says [Sam. I 26:19], "They have driven me out this day that I should not cleave to the inheritance of Hashem, saying 'Go, serve other gods.'" When the Torah tells us, "and you shall place these words upon your heart" [Deut. 11:18], this tells us we are to keep bodily obligations like *tefillin* and *mezuza* outside the Land, but only in order that the commandments not be new to us when we return. For the essence of all the commandments is reserved for the dwellers of the Land

the Land it is as if he has departed the domain of the Holy One, blessed be He, God forbid.

---

of Hashem. Therefore, Sifre [Re'e 80] states, "you will inherit it, and live in it, and guard the commandments" [Deut. 11:31–32] implies the settlement of the Land of Israel is equal to all the commandments in the Torah.

SARAI'S YUD IS TRANSFERRED TO HOSHEA

17:15. You shall not call her name Sarai, for Sara is her name.

Rashi on 17:5: The yud *of Sarai complained to the Heavenly Presence until He added it to Yehoshua's name, as it says [Num. 13:16], "and Moshe called Hoshea the son of Nun, Yehoshua."*

Gur Arye: This is the midrash: The *yud* said, "Because I am the smallest of the letters You took me from the name of the righteous woman." Said Hashem: "You started at the end of a female's name and now you will be at the beginning of a male's name, as it says [Num. 13:16], 'And Moshe called Hoshea, the son of Nun, Yehoshua.'" The Torah is established for eternity and never changes,[16] for it transcends worldly limitations.[17] The *yud* is so small, it too is not subject to change,[18] especially in conjunction with the name of a righteous person.[19] For all these reasons, the *yud* objected to being removed from Sarai's name.

Now, let us consider the meaning and the various linguistic applications of the *yud*. Because it cannot be reduced or subdivided, it connotes unity. Moshe wanted Yehoshua to be complete unto himself, not cancelled out by the large number who opposed him.[20] At the end of a word, the *yud* connotes limitation, as Sarai

---

16. Tiferet Yisrael 49:152b: Just as it is impossible to change anything Hashem created, it is impossible to change one word of the Torah. Therefore the midrash says [Sh. ha-Sh. Rab. on 5:11]: If everyone in the world came to whiten the raven's wing, they could not do it. Similarly, if everyone in the world came to uproot a single small word from the Torah, they could not do it.

17. Tiferet Yisrael 50:155b: The Torah is from the upper world and not subject to worldly limitation and *shinui* [change, departure from order]. Torah does not come from man. See introduction to Derech Hachaim, 7b.

18. See Netiv Hatorah 1, 1:3b, Or Chadash 62a, and others.

19. See Chidushei Agadot on Sanh. 70a, 3:176a; Gur Arye 23:1[2]; and Netiv Hatzedek 2, 2:137a–140b.

20. Tiferet Yisrael 49:153b.

was princess only to her people. Replacing the *yud* with a *heh* expanded her dominion to the whole world. At the beginning of a word, the *yud* connotes expansion, growth, and strength. A *yud* at the beginning of the name of a male raises his level, while it is improper to have a female name begin with this letter for it conflicts with her modesty, although there are many exceptions.[21]

Avraham and Sara were to become the foundation stones for the people of Israel. The *yud,* which was so small and cast off from Sarai's name, was to confer leadership to Yehoshua and a new beginning for the people of Israel on their own Land.

---

21. Netiv Hatzeniut 1, 2:106b and Chidushei Agadot on Kid. 49b, 2:157a.

AVRAHAM'S PLEA AND YISHMAEL'S FREE CHOICE

> 17:18. And Avraham said to Hashem: "O that Yishmael might live before You!"

Rashi: "Live before You" means live in fear of You, just as "Walk before Me" [17:1] means, as rendered by Onkelos, worship before Me.

Gur Arye: Avraham might have said, "O that Yishmael might live!" The verse is complete without "before You," and so another meaning is being conveyed, "in fear of You." Ramban is troubled that Hashem should answer: "With respect to Yishmael, I have heard you" [17:20] implying that Avraham's wish was fulfilled. Not only does this violate "All is in the hands of heaven except the fear of heaven" [Ber. 33b], but it did not even come to pass, as Yishmael committed the three cardinal sins [Rashi 21:9] and did not repent till the end of his days [Rashi 25:9].

To answer Ramban, look carefully at the previous Rashi – Avraham asked only that Yishmael live, as his deeds depend on himself and not on Hashem. Avraham's request was that Yishmael be allowed to live to have the opportunity to serve and fear Hashem. Hashem answered in the affirmative – yes, he will be allowed to live.

MDK: Ramban's objection to Rashi is the apparent request to suspend Yishmael's free will, a request subsequently granted by Hashem. Gur Arye answers that Avraham's request was limited to allowing Yishmael to live.

YITZCHAK'S NAME

17:19. And you shall call his name Yitzchak…

Rashi: Yitzchak is on account of the laughter, and on account of the ten [yud] tests and the ninety [tzadi] years of Sara and the eight [chet] days of the circumcision and the hundred [kuf] years of Avraham.

Gur Arye: Rashi brings two reasons for the name Yitzchak. Since the name means laughter, it connotes his parents' response to the news of his impending arrival. Additionally, the four letters of the name correspond to four numbers associated with Yitzchak's birth.

One must ask, what do the ten tests have to do with Yitzchak's birth? The answer is that they call attention to the challenge, to the relevant test, the circumcision, posed to Avraham. Hashem wanted Avraham to be circumcised before Yitzchak was conceived.[22] Hashem also made the test more difficult by waiting till Avraham was old. When he passes the test and circumcises himself and the male members of his household, he is miraculously rewarded at the age of 100, and his wife at the age of 90, with Yitzchak, who is circumcised on the eighth day. Now all the elements of the acronym come together.

---

22. Ramban 17:4 quotes Ibn Ezra: Blessed is Hashem who first commanded Avraham to enter the covenant of circumcision before Sara conceived, in order that his seed be holy. Rashi, Shab. 137b, on the blessing recited at the brit, "who sanctified the beloved one from the womb": This is Yitzchak, for before he was born he was sanctified for this commandment [17:19]. See also Chidushei Agadot ad loc. 1:70a and Pachad Yitzchak, Succot, Yerech Etanim 5: Avraham and Yaakov had their names changed but not Yitzchak. Avraham's patriarchy was that he was the first of converts, and Yitzchak's patriarchy was that he was the first sanctified from the womb, thus becoming the first circumcised on the eighth day. The latter was born with his patriarchy, so he needed no name change.

MDK: What is troubling Gur Arye? It is not apparent what the number ten has to do with Yitzchak. He answers that ten calls attention to the ten tests Avraham underwent, resulting in the focus on circumcision.

THE PATRIARCHS ARE THE HOLY CHARIOT

> 17:22. And He finished speaking to him, and
> Hashem arose from upon Avraham.

Rashi: This language is respectful to the Divine Presence [Mizrachi: for without the "upon" one could imagine Hashem and Avraham to have been at the same level.] Additionally, it teaches us that the righteous ones constitute the Chariot of the Holy One, blessed be He.

Gur Arye: The respectful language refers to arising from a level higher than where Avraham was standing, if one could say this about the Divine Presence. The reason for the Chariot is that the righteous bring the Divine Presence down to earth [BR 19:7].[23] Rabbi Shimon bar Yochai learned, "everywhere the righteous go the Divine Presence is upon them" [BR 86:6].

MDK: Two images are projected to physically describe where God was in relation to Avraham. Me'al can mean "above" or "from over." The simplest image is the Shechina hovering above Avraham, from whence It departed. The first midrash suggests that out of respect, the verse disguises the real relationship, which was, so to speak, on level ground. The image of the second midrash has Hashem riding on Avraham's back, in the sense that the patriarchs brought the knowledge of Hashem and His Torah to this world.

---

23. Num. R. 13:2: The righteous ones cause the Divine Presence to dwell on earth. See also the converse in Gur Arye 6:9[15].

Vayera

THE SECRET OF THE KOMATZ

18:3. And he said, *Adonoi* [my lords or, alternatively, God], if it please you that I find favor in your eyes, please do not pass from before your servant.

Rashi: First he called them all lords, then he singled out the greatest of them to stay, for that would result in the others staying. This interprets adonoi *in the ordinary sense of "my lords." Alternatively, the term is [a reference to the] sacred, and he was asking the Holy One, blessed be He, to wait while he ushered in the visitors.*

Gur Arye: Rashi addresses the change in the verse from plural, lords, to singular *taavor*, pass. Now one must ask, the plural is usually expressed with the *patach*, which should be read as *adonai* rather than *adonoi*. Rabbenu Bechaye notes that the *komatz* [vowel sounded o in the Ashkenazi accent] means both singular and plural, as the form of the notation shows – the *komatz* is a dash with a teardrop underneath. It is thus a grafting of a *patach*, denoting plural, and *chirik*, denoting singular. The *komatz* is a literary device peculiar to the Hebrew tongue that conveys singular and plural simultaneously.

Now consider *Adonoi* in the sacred sense. The *chirik* part of the *komatz*, the dot in the teardrop, addresses His Oneness, my singular Master. However, to address Hashem in the singular

(*Adoni*) would lack the proper respect due Him. The *patach* part of the *komatz* conveys the proper decorum [the royal plural, thee instead of you, *Ihr* instead of *du* (German). *Adonoi* addresses both His Oneness and the proper decorum.

How did Avraham know which of the three men was the greatest? The rabbis said [Yom. 37a] if a teacher and his students are walking together, the students walk at his side. However, it is forbidden to walk directly behind or directly at the side. The proper way is to the side and a little to the back. This is how he knew.

MDK: The proper written rendition of the komatz *would appear to be the teardrop rather than the* T. *The Ashkenazic spoken rendition makes a distinction between* adonai *and* adonoi *which the Sephardic does not, but I have noted many who speak with a Sephardic pronunciation make an exception in the case of God's name and say* Adonoi.

THE LOGIC OF IDOLATRY

18:5. Let some water be brought and wash your feet.

Rashi: He presumed they were Arabs who bowed down to the dust of their feet...

Gur Arye: There are those who ask [Mizrachi's question] how they could have deified the dust of their feet! This midrash should not trouble us in light of "Zevuv [fly], the god of Ekron" [Kings II 1:3] – *they bowed down to a fly!* Why did they fear a fly? The answer is that idolaters have corrupted their understanding, thinking Hashem is too holy to worship.[1] Everything in the lower sphere has a power that rules it in the upper sphere. They choose unholy powers to be their deities, powers who rule lesser things. Man is the highest entity in the lower sphere, and the closest entity to him in the upper sphere is the power that rules the lowliest. Therefore, Ekron worships the lord of a fly and the Arab worships the lord of the dust, the lowliest entities in their world.

Also, Arabs wander from place to place and do not settle a place for themselves – they are tent dwellers.[2] They always have dust on their feet and bow down to it, saying they are subservient to the angel who rules the road. Those who worship Aries, the sheep constellation, worship animals.[3] Likewise the Arabs, who worship the *mazal* of the road, bow down to the dust of the road.

---

1. Rambam, Guide to the Perplexed 1:38 and Yad Hachazaka, Laws of Idolatry.
2. BR 55:9: "And he will be a wild man" [16:12] means that whereas everyone else grows up in a settled area, he grows up in the desert. See Rashi 16:12 and 21:20.
3. R.H. 11a: *Mazal Tele* [Aries] corresponds to the month of Nisan, when animals, beasts, and fowl mate.

A PRESUMPTION OF RIGHTEOUSNESS

> 18:5. I will get a morsel of bread that you may
> nourish your heart [*libchem*].

Rashi: ...Rabbi Chama said it is not written levavchem [*your {plural} hearts*] *but rather* libchem [*your {plural} heart*]. *This tells us that the evil inclination holds no sway over angels.*

Gur Arye: This Rashi can be understood in conjunction with his comment on [Deut. 6:2], "And you shall love Hashem, your God, with all your heart [*levavchem*]." What does the second *bet* in *levavchem* convey? Both inclinations, the good and the evil, must love Hashem. Here, the heart of each angel is singular.

But Avraham thought the angels were men! How could he attribute to them the absence of an evil inclination? I think Avraham wanted to speak an honorable expression to the visitors. Giving them the benefit of the doubt, he assumed their good inclination dominated their evil inclination. This depite the rabbis injunction [B.B. 12b] that man has two hearts, and despite his assumption that they were sand worshipers. This speaks to the character of this great patriarch.

It is possible that this expression was an inadvertent prophecy,[4] that at some level of consciousness he knew they were angels.

MDK: Avraham's tendency to give everyone the benefit of the doubt can be viewed as a beautiful character trait or a flaw in his understanding of human nature. He exhibits it in defence of Sedom and again in defence of Yishmael.

---

4.   B.B. 119b: In the Song of the Sea, Moshe and the children of Israel say, "Bring them and plant them on the mountain of their inheritance" [Ex. 15:17] – it does not say "bring us." This comes to teach us that Moshe and the children of Israel were giving us a prophecy not knowing that it was prophecy.

THE THREE APPROACHES TO HASHEM – THE SECRET OF THE GREAT, THE MIGHTY, AND THE AWESOME

18:23. And Avraham approached and said, Will You obliterate even righteous with wicked?

Rashi: We find the expression hagasha [*approach*] *used for war – "And Yoav approached...for war"* [Chron. 1 19:14]; *for conciliation – "And Yehuda approached him"* [44:18]; *and for prayer – "And Eliahu approached..."* [Kings 1 18:36]. *Avraham undertook all three – to speak with toughness* [war], *with* piyus [*submission, appeasement*], *and with prayer.*

Gur Arye: Avraham begins his dialogue with Hashem by confronting Him with the unfairness of killing the righteous along with the wicked. The right is on his side and he wants justice. This tough language is called "war."[5] He then uses an expression of *piyus* [submission, appeasement] – "and I am dust and ashes" [18:27]. Then he prays – "please, do not become angry with Your servant" [18:30]. This prayer, as all prayers, is a request to bypass Judgment and act out of Mercy.[6] It seems to me that Avraham has a single goal – to save Sedom, and he attempts to reach it by three different routes.

This midrash [BR 49:8] hints at a most hidden matter. With his three approaches, Avraham addressed the three names of God – *El*, *Elokim*, and YKVK. Addressing Elokim, which is the Attribute of Judgment, he spoke harshly – that is the war route. Addressing *El*, which is the Attribute of Kindness[7], he spoke submissively,

---

5. Ramban: It is impossible through the Attribute of Judgment to kill the righteous with the wicked, for the people would say, "the worship of *Elokim* is in vain" [Mal. 3:14].

6. Netiv Hateshuva 6, 2:164a: That He is merciful means He does not exact the letter of the law and allows His creatures to live. Prayer is intended to cancel punishment imposed by judgment by invoking mercy.

7. See Rashi, Deut. 3:24. Your Greatness is Your Goodness.

trying to conciliate. Self-effacement and humility serve to aggrandize the object of one's plea. This name is Supreme Kindness, the source of all good that He does for His creatures.[8] Addressing YKVK, the Attribute of Mercy, he prayed for mercy.[9]

When, in the Amida, we say "the Great, the Strong, and the Awesome" [from Deut. 10:17] we invoke Avraham's three approaches. Righteous indignation, or "war," is addressed to "the Strong," the Attribute of Judgment.[10] Submission is addressed to "the Great," the Attribute of Kindness.[11] Prayer is addressed to "the Awesome,"[12] the Attribute of Mercy.

MDK: Since Avraham's "approach" does not apply in a physical sense, Rashi's citations show us three unanticipated meanings that teach us ways to relate to Hashem, each of which we invoke in the Amida.

Approach:	Submission	War	Prayer
Target:	El	Elokim	YKVK
Description:	Great	Strong	Awesome
Attribute:	Kindness	Judgment	Mercy
Patriarch:	Avraham	Yitzchak	Yaakov

---

8. Ibid: The *Gemara* does not explain the meaning of El...It seems this name refers to *chesed* [kindness] as in [Ps. 22:2], "My El, my El, why have you forsaken me?" See Derech Hachaim on 1:2 and Gur Arye, Ex. 34:6: El is an extra measure of goodness and kindness that He gives man, whereas *YKVK* does only what the person needs. Netzach Yisrael 47:166b: The difference between El and *YKVK* is the difference between kindness and mercy. Kindness is gratuitous, undeserved good provided to the world. Mercy is what is given when there is distress in the lower spheres. Also see 30:3[7].

9. BR 33:3 and 1:1[16], and Ex. R. 3:6: When I have mercy on my world I am called *YKVK*, for *YKVK* is the Attribute of Mercy.

10. See Gevurot Hashem, Intro. 3:19 and Netiv Ha'avoda 12, 1:115a.

11. Rashi, Deut 3:24: "Your greatness is the attribute of Your kindness." Also Gur Arye, 12:2[5].

12. See Netiv Yirat Hashem 5, 2:34b and Netiv Ha'avoda 3, 1:82a: Prayer is called service, for man depends on Him, and needs Him, and cannot survive without Him. This dependency generates awe.

THE SECRET OF LOT'S REWARD

19:29. …and God remembered Avraham, and He
sent Lot out from the midst of the upheaval…

*Rashi: What remembrance of Avraham pertaining to Lot is referred
to here? Lot, knowing Sara was Avraham's wife, overheard him say
in Egypt, "she is my sister" [12:19]. Lot did not reveal the matter,
for he had pity on his uncle. Therefore the Holy One, blessed be He,
had pity on Lot.*

Gur Arye: Mizrachi is troubled by Rashi's question. Is it not obvious that Avraham loved Lot in that he pursued the kings [14:14] on his account and put his life in danger? Furthermore, Lot left his homeland and birthplace to go with Avraham [12:4]. All of these are "remembrances of Avraham" that are credits to Lot. Why abandon all these reasons for an esoteric event, the keeping of a secret that, had it been revealed, would have resulted in Avraham's death?

The difficulty is resolved considering the opinion of the rabbis [BR 51:6] that Mizrachi's suggestions are not remembrances of Avraham that accrue to Lot's credit. Familial relationships only accrue benefits to fathers and sons, as in "He remembers the kindness of the fathers"[13] and "a son gives merit to his father" [Sanh. 104a]. In Lot's case, not only was he just a nephew, but a nephew who distanced himself from his uncle, saying "I cannot abide Avraham and his God" [Rashi 13:11]. When Lot left his homeland to go with Avraham, it was for his own benefit. Whatever attachment to Avraham Lot initially had was severed when he left his uncle and renounced whatever merit he accrued. By default, Lot's keeping Avraham's secret is his only merit. This is the revealed [*nigla*] answer.

---

13. From the Amida prayer. Also Yitzchak merited his father's credits [26:5] and Shlomo merited David's [Kings I 3:14].

The midrash that Lot remained silent knowing Avraham's secret hints at a mystical secret hidden in the Torah. The sages said [BR 41:6] that Lot's face was just like his uncle's [Rashi 13:8], meaning Lot had an inner connection and relationship with Avraham, as *panim* [face] means *penim* [inside, inherent character]. His silence prepared him to later be considered as Avraham's son [Rashi, Deut. 2:5]. In the *nigla* [revealed, non-mystical], Lot separated from Avraham, but in the *nistar* [hidden, mystical], there was an inner bond between the two, for *panim* [face] comes from *penim* [inner].[14] By keeping Avraham's secret,[15] he established a relationship with his internal essence [*penimiuto*], which explains Rashi's comment [Deut. 2:5], "He made Lot to be like a son."[16]

The *Talmud* says [B.K. 38b] that from the two good doves, the daughters of Lot, Hashem wanted to bring forth the kingdom of the House of David.[17] Why should Amon and Moav specifically be the progenitors of the Messiah? Lot had within him a drop of holiness that came from being the nephew of Avraham. But this drop was mixed with poison such that Lot could not abide with Avraham till the drop was cleansed and purified and Hashem

---

14. B.M. 59a: A man's face influences his level in the World to Come. Chidushei Agadot, ad. loc: It is known that in the World to Come there is an inner secret – to whiten someone's face [to embarrass him] causes a high level defect internally [*bifnim*].

15. Gur Arye, Ex. 2:14 on Rashi's note, that when Moshe saw there were evil talebearers in Israel he said, perhaps Israel is not fit to be redeemed. It is an exalted inner level [of the Israelites] that is not revealed [to the open eye] which brings about their redemption. He who reveals it, reverses it, for he cleaves to the low level called external and revealed. Therefore, as long as there are talebearers in Israel, bondage is appropriate for them. The redemption proves Israel is at the highest, innermost secret level.

16. Gur Arye, Num. 16:1[4]: Certainly, when righteous bear wicked children, it shows there are inner defects in the righteous, for every righteous person has defects from which the wicked offspring can derive. Ramban, Deut. 29:17: The father is the root of the son...a sweet root cannot bring forth bitterness, and he whose heart is *shalem* [harmoniously complete] with Hashem cannot think idolatrous thoughts.

17. See Gur Arye, Num. 31:2[1], Yeb. 77a, and BR 41:4.

grafted it upon Israel through Rut the Moavite and Naama the Amonite. In the end, the drop will be further purified until from it will come the King, Messiah [Netzach Yisrael 32:149b].

MDK: Gur Arye juxtaposes the revealed and the hidden. In the former, keeping the secret is a default justification for saving Lot. In the latter, the secret is a window to the mysteries of Lot's inner relationship with Avraham that would propel his role in Jewish destiny.

SARA'S HOLY SPIRIT

> 21:12. …All that Sara says to you – listen to her voice [*kol*].

Rashi: We learned that Avraham had a lower level of prophecy as compared to Sara.

Gur Arye: *Ruach* means both wind and spirit and the voice is not heard without it. The *ruach* of Sara's voice was the Holy Spirit [*Ruach Hakodesh*]. We saw this earlier, when Sara suggested her husband take a concubine, "and Avram listened to the voice of Sarai" [16:2], upon which Rashi comments that her "voice" referred to the Holy Spirit within her. This means he heard the part of her that was the Holy Spirit itself. We know from the Ten Commandments [Deut. 4:12] that voice [*kol*] means the Holy Spirit, where Hashem spoke to them from the midst of the fire – "you were hearing the sound [*kol*] of words and you did not see the picture, only the *kol*."[18] The voice of Sara was the voice of the Holy Spirit.

MDK: Hashem instructs Avraham to consider Sara's voice as the Holy Spirit itself. The higher reaches of her soul cleave to Him in such a way that her voice is His voice.

---

18. See also 26:5[4], Num. 21:35[33], and Or Chadash 113a.

YISHMAEL'S PRAYER IS ANSWERED

21:17. And Hashem heard the voice of the youth.

Rashi: From here we learn that the prayer of a sick person is pre-ferred to the prayers of others on his behalf, and will be the first accepted.

Gur Arye: The *Talmud* relates [Ber. 5b] the case of Rabbi Yochanan who was ill and who had Rabbi Chanina help heal him by holding his hand. The question is posed there – why did Rabbi Yochanan not heal himself? The answer is given – a prisoner cannot release himself from prison. This principle seems to conflict with Yishmael's experience here.

The answer in the prayer context differs from the healing context. The sick person, like the prisoner, is limited in what he can accomplish on his own behalf. With the aid of another he can rally to save himself. Rabbi Chanina was helping Rabbi Yochanan help himself so as to deserve Hashem's help. When Yishmael prayed for himself, he was doomed and only Hashem could save him. He could not have helped himself with the aid of others as did the prisoner or the sick person. In such a desperate state, his only hope was miraculous divine intervention. Although in the previous verse his mother prayed for him, it was *his* prayers that were heard and answered.

THE ORCHARD AND THE INN

21:33. And he planted an *eshel* [terebinth] in Be'er Sheva.

Rashi: Rav and Shmuel disputed the meaning of this. One said it was an orchard to provide wayfarers with fruit. One said it was an inn in which were all kinds of foods. We find the verb "to plant" applies to tents, as in [Dan. 11:45]: "And he will plant the tents of his palace."

Gur Arye: What difference does it make [whether it was an] orchard or an inn? Two theories are hinted at. An orchard – planted trees – befits Avraham in that he was the first *netia* [sapling, planting], the source of divine inspiration for the world.[19] On his account the world was created, as it is written [2:4], "This is the story of heaven and earth when they were created [*b'hibaream*]," which the midrash [BR 12:9] transposes to "*b'Avraham*," which is interpreted to mean "on account of Avraham."[20] There had been 2000 years of *tohu* [confusion][21] and the world as we know it came into existence when Hashem planted His first *netia* [seedling], Avraham.[22] That is why the orchard befits him, a blessing in the world

---

19. Derech Hachaim, intro. 7b: The Torah is called "tree" for it is a strong planting with deep roots. All the winds in the world, [all the movements through history], do not move it from its place. If one should try to uproot the Torah, he could not move a single word.
20. Netiv Ha'avoda 4, 1:86b: Avraham is the essential, the beginning, the first of the world, having a special place next to Hashem. He is strong like a tree, with deep roots such that the winds cannot move him from his place. See Derech Hachaim 5:3, 224b.
21. A.Z. 9a: The world was designed to exist for 6000 years, 2000 years of *tohu*, 2000 years of Torah, 2000 years of redemption. 2000 years of Torah began… when Avraham was 52. See Gevurot Hashem 5, 32a.
22. See Chidushei Agadot on A.Z. 9a; Gevurot Hashem 9, 53b and 2:16[17].

from which all benefit.[23] According to the view that *eshel* is an inn, it relates to Avraham's inn, where wayfarers gathered; thus he was called "the father of many nations" [17:5].[24] He and his inn allowed for a continuation of the sustenance of his guests.[25]

The foundation or planting of wisdom is called "orchard" [Hag. 14b], a planting that gives forth fruit. Avraham's planting was the orderly setting forth of wisdom – strong roots of truth which all could agree to. If someone wished to grasp a concept, Avraham would bring it to him out of his orchard. The fruit that is wisdom causes the recipient to beget further, secondary fruit when the seeds are planted.[26]

The "inn" view differs from the "orchard" view in the nature of the information he imparted to people. Instead of wisdom, the "inn" view has it that he taught them how to behave, that is, which deeds are acceptable to Hashem. This is how he brought all the wayfarers, great and small, intelligent and dull, under the wings of the Divine Presence [Rashi 12:5]. The midrash has it that Avraham says, "Ask what you want – bread, meat, wine, eggs," for good deeds are the life force and the ongoing survival for the soul,[27] the same way that food sustains the body. Processed foods are specified rather than fruit, to show that effort is required. Bread and meat are specified for they sustain the body,[28] unlike fruit, which pleases without sustaining. The Torah says with respect to deeds,

---

23. BR 54:6: Rabbi Yehuda says *eshel* is an orchard – ask for what you wish, figs, grapes, pomegranates...

24. BR 39:3: "We have a small sister" [s.o.s. 8:8] refers to the guests of Avraham, who was a brother to everyone in the world. Radal explains that he enlightened his guests to unify their hearts to their Father in heaven.

25. Derech Hachaim 5:8, 243b: The reason he who separates *chala* is blessed is that *chala* is a commandment pertaining to the house, meaning the sustenance of the house, as we say "the blessing of the house" [Ket. 103a].

26. Hag. 3b: A planting reproduces just as words of Torah reproduce.

27. See Gur Arye 6:9[16], Netiv Hatorah 7, 1:31a and 17, 1:72a, and Derech Hachaim 1:17, 55a.

28. Tos., Ber. 41b [*Hilchata*]: Foods that are not eaten in the main part of the meal, like dates, pomegranates, and other fruits, do not sustain. Shab. 129a: What

"and live by them" [Lev. 18:5], for the deeds are the most important, more important than learning.[29] If man would be completely spiritual, his Torah would be most important, as learning is done by the *sechel* [intelligence, spirituality]. But since he is partially physical, deeds take precedence, and deeds are functions of the body.

MDK: Both explanations of Avraham's contribution to mankind, the orchard and the inn, are true. He brought wisdom to the world, but more importantly, he brought ethics to the world.[30]

To summarize:

	Orchard	*Inn*
Origin:	*planted*	*erected*
Content:	*information*	*ethics*
Target:	*the wise*	*everyone*
Menu:	*figs, pomegranates*	*bread, eggs, meat*
	delicacies	*basic nutrition*
	natural	*processed*
	satisfies	*sustains*
Goal:	*wisdom*	*good deeds*

---

is required for a sustaining meal? Bread and wine. See Derech Hachaim 5:8, 241b.

29. Chidushei Agadot on Kid. 40a, 2:143b.
30. See Cahill, T. *The Gifts of the Jews*. New York: Anchor Press, 1998.

Chayei Sara

THE HIDDEN MEANING OF ELIEZER'S GIFTS

24:22. And the man took a gold nose ring weighing a *beka*, and two bracelets for her arms weighing ten gold shekels.

Rashi: Beka [half shekel] *is an allusion to the "beka per head" donation to the Tabernacle* [Ex. 38:26], *two bracelets allude to the two tablets of the covenant, and ten shekels to the Ten Commandments upon them.*

Gur Arye: The midrash quoted by Rashi [BR 60:16] is derived from the apparently superfluous detail of the description of the gifts. Why allude to something Rivka could not possibly understand? The answer is, though she could not understand, her *mazal* [celestial counterpart] could [Meg. 3a]. He hinted at this commandment, the donation for the offerings, because he saw her to be a person of kind deeds [Rashi 24:14]. Also, the *beka* was used for the service of Hashem in the Holy Tabernacle. The two bracelets hinted at the two tablets with the Ten Commandments representing the Torah.[1] Now we have Shimon Hatzadik's three pillars on which ·

---

1. Derech Hachaim 1:2, 29a: The sacrifices produced a "pleasant aroma" [Ex. 29:25], hinted at by the nose ring, for the nose senses aroma. Similarly, the arms represent the tablets as it is written, "the two tablets were in his two arms" [Deut. 9:15].

the world stands – Torah, Service, and Good Deeds [Avot. 1:2]. Once he witnessed her good deeds, one of the pillars, he hinted to her that she could merit the other two.

MDK: The midrash addresses the elaborate description of Eliezer's gifts to Rivka. Since there is no unnecessary or superfluous word or even letter in the Torah, an explanation is called for.

THE BLESSINGS OF SARA

24:67. And Yitzchak brought her to the tent of
Sara his mother…

Rashi: He brought her to the tent, and she was "Sara, his mother,"
that is to say, the image of Sara, his mother. For all the time Sara
was alive, a lamp would be lit from Sabbath eve to Sabbath eve, and
blessing would be found in the dough, and a cloud would be bound
over the tent. When she died, they stopped, and when Rivka came,
they returned [BR 60:16].

Gur Arye: Rashi cites three commandments, corresponding to
the three incumbent on women cited by the Mishna.[2] "Blessing
is found in the dough" corresponds to *chala* [separation of part
of the dough to be given to the cohen].[3] "Lit light" refers to the
commandment of lighting Sabbath lights. "A cloud bound to the
tent" is the Cloud of Honor, which is the Divine Presence, honoring Sara's holiness and purity,[4] for purity brings the Holy Spirit.[5]
Since Sara observed the laws of purity and menstrual separation,
she merited the Cloud of Honor on her tent.

The same midrash [BR 60:17] brings a fourth merit of Sara,
that her house was always open. Rashi omits this, as it does not

---

2. Shab. 31b: For three transgressions women die during childbirth – for not
   observing carefully family purity, *chala*, and lighting Shabbat candles.
3. Ezek. 44:30: The first of your dough you shall give to the *cohen* to place blessing on your house. Derech Hachaim 5:8, 243b: Why the blessing for *chala*? For
   chala is a commandment relating to the house, the sustenance of the house…
   thus the house is blessed. See Ket. 103a.
4. Netzach Yisrael 4, 19a: The first Holy Temple had a unique attribute – the
   Divine Presence resided there. Its destruction ensued when it became unfit
   for the Divine Presence, that is, when it became *tamei* [ritually impure] and
   Hashem does not dwell amidst impurity…The three cardinal sins are called
   "impurity," thus the Temple was destroyed.
5. A.Z. 20b: Purity brings holiness, holiness brings humility, humility brings fear
   of sin, fear of sin brings saintliness, and saintliness brings the Holy Spirit.

fit the *Mishna*. However, the author of the midrash is cognizant of another correspondence – the four corners of the *Merkava* [Holy Chariot, Hashem's throne].[6] These are Avraham, Yitzchak, Yaakov, David. "The cloud bound to the tent" is Avraham's attribute, kindness.[7] The "blessing found in dough" relates to Yitzchak [Rashi 12:2].[8] The "door open wide" relates to Yaakov through whom *revacha* [width, plenty] comes to the world.[9] The "lit lamp" relates to David as we say in the *haftara* blessing, "his lamp will not go out forever," and in the Amida of the Days of Awe, "the setting of a lamp for Yishai's son, Your anointed one."[10] All the words of our sages are precise in their wisdom, not to be added to, nor diminished from.

MDK: Maharal chides Rashi for omitting the fourth leg of the midrash he cites. At the same time, the rationale of Rashi's choice, that it conforms to the Mishna *that brings the commandments relating to women, is clearly stated. The author of the Midrash seems to want the Chariot to represent both Sara's blessing and the "four"*

6. Gevurot Hashem 47:167b: The four corners represent wisdom, strength, wealth, and honor, corresponding to the lion, the ox, the eagle, and man. See Zohar 3, 257b and Gur Arye, Num. 4:13.

7. See 24:22[17]{97} and Netzach Yisrael 54, 201a.

8. See 12:2[5] and 21:1[2].

9. Isa. 58:14: …then you will have pleasure with comfort through Hashem…and he will feed you the inheritance of Yaakov. See Shab. 118a. Or Chadash 154a: "*Revach* [width, plenty] and rescue will arise for the Jews from another place" [Est. 4:14], for Israel's place is their father Yaakov, who is their source…and because the blessing of Yaakov is boundless, as it is written, "You will break out to the West, the East, the North, and the South." See 27:28[15].

10. Derasha Leshabbat Hagadol 224b: David is counted among the patriarchs of the world because his attribute is a mix of the three of them. Derech Hachaim 4:14, 169a: The crown of priesthood is bodily [*guf*] holiness, the crown of kingship is spiritual [*nefesh*] holiness, the crown of Torah is intellectual [*sechel*] holiness, and the crown of a good name corresponds to the essence of the man. The *menora* [lamp] hints at the crown of a good name.

patriarchs. It is even possible that Rashi chooses to omit part of the Midrash because he also finds it a stretch to fit four patriarchs into Sara's attributes.

Toldot

THE ETERNAL STRUGGLE THAT
BEGAN IN RIVKA'S WOMB

25:22. And the children thrashed within her…

Netzach Yisrael 15:87b: When Esav requested Yaakov's lentil soup, Yaakov made him a proposition. Our rabbis[1] interpret the verse, "Sell me *kayom* [like the day] your birthright" [25:31] to mean, like the time you and I [Esav and Yaakov] were inside their mother's womb. Said Yaakov to Esav, "My brother, there are two worlds before us, this one and the World to Come. This world has eating and drinking, business, marrying a woman, having children. The World to Come has none of that. If you want, you take this world and I the other, just as we discussed [*kayom*] in our mother's womb." At that moment, Esav renounced the resurrection of souls and said, "I am about to die, why should I need a birthright?" [25:32]. At that point, Esav took his portion in this world and Yaakov took his portion in the World to Come. Many years later, Esav sees Yaakov return from Lavan with family and material possessions and says, "My brother, this was not the deal! You are getting this world, too! Let us make a partnership and share both worlds." Yaakov spurns his brother, as it is written [33:13], "The children are tender and the flocks and cattle are my responsibility, and driving them hard [to keep up with you] will cause them to die."

---

1. Yalkut Shimoni 1:111 and Tana Devei Eliahu Zuta 19.

If you should ask, "This is too fanciful – how can fetuses speak to each other in the womb? They have no opinions, no will, no inclinations to good or evil [8:21{24}]!" The answer is that a fetus has potential [*koach*], and it was their potentials that opposed each other. Yaakov's *koach* was holiness – Esav's *koach* was the opposite, impurity, and poison. Yaakov was spiritual, devoid of physicality – Esav was limited to the physical, devoid of spirituality. Such opposites cannot occupy the same domain.

If you should ask, "What is the problem? Let Esav occupy this physical world and Yaakov occupy the spiritual World to Come – then there would be no 'thrashing'!" The answer is that both brothers wanted both worlds. Consider that a person, and correspondingly the world, has three domains – *guf* [body, physical self], *nefesh* [fusion of worldly body and heavenly soul], and *sechel hanivdal* [transcendent spiritual self]. Hashem in his wisdom ceded *guf* to Esav and *sechel hanivdal* to Yaakov. Thus far there is no struggle, for the two opposites occupy separate domains. But both brothers lay claim to the middle ground – the *nefesh* – and the eternal struggle begins.

The three domains are compared to the sequential stages of the life of a person. From birth he finds himself in a totally physical world [*guf*]. He screams immediately and is put to the breast. His physical needs are constant, his total preoccupation. Later, his rewards and punishments are physical, and later still, in adolescence, his body image becomes his preoccupation. Then, he acquires a measure of spirituality and passes to adulthood and its attendant responsibilities – self-sustenance, family building, work, relationships. These responsibilities are mostly physical and preclude spiritual attainments, resulting in the *nefesh* stage, a stalemate between the physical and the spiritual. In later years, he loses his powers, and the physical pursuits have less and less relevance to him. He passes to the *sechel* stage and becomes progressively spiritual, eventually shedding the trappings of this world totally.

The womb similarly has three domains – the lower segment where the fetus dwells the first trimester, the middle segment where he dwells the second trimester, and the upper segment where he dwells the third trimester. Consider two rocks in a bottle. The first rock in goes to the bottom of the bottle, the next rock takes its place above it. The seed that fertilized Yaakov's zygote entered the womb first, and that zygote was implanted high in the womb. Esav's zygote was then implanted in the lower segment. The rest is history.

MDK: I selected the version of the Yaakov/ Esav struggle found in Netzach Yisrael, the Maharal's treatise on exile and redemption, because it deals globally with the subject and is much more colorful than the Gur Arye. It pulls together three events, the struggle in the womb, the selling of the birthright, and the reunion of the brothers after twenty-seven years, and sets the stage for Esav's dominance through the exile and his ultimate submission in the end of days.

DID THE PATRIARCHS KEEP THE COMMANDMENTS?

26:5. Because Avraham heard my voice [*kol*]…

Rashi: When I tested him.

Gur Arye: *Kol* [sound, voice] means something other than words. It means he did not carefully consider Hashem's words, but accepted them unconditionally. Similarly, "If you will hear the *kol* of Hashem, your God…all the illness I placed upon Egypt I will not place upon you" [Ex. 15:26] is a warning not to ponder and consider whether [or not] to do the commands of Hashem.[2] The ten trials of Avraham [Ab. 5:3] are referred to here and not the laws of the Torah, which Hashem did not command him to keep.

26:5. …and observed My safeguards, My commandments, My decrees, and My teachings.

Rashi: These "safeguards" are rabbinical laws instituted for keeping a distance from transgressions of Torah prohibitions, such as secondary [rabbinical] sexual prohibitions and rabbinical Sabbath prohibitions that serve to place a fence around the Torah. The "commandments" are items that, even had they not been written, it would be appropriate to include them in a code of law, like thievery and murder. "Decrees" refer to items that the evil inclination and the other nations of the world taunt us about, like the prohibitions of eating pork and wearing sha'atnez [a word which etymologically means "smoothed, twined, and woven," but is used to refer to a combination of linen and wool]. "Teachings" are the Oral Law, given to Moshe at Sinai.

Gur Arye: It seems counter-intuitive for Rashi to place the

---

2. See 16:2[3] and 21:12[14].

distancing rabbinical laws ahead of the commandments of the Torah! To understand this, consider that rabbinical laws are man-made, and therefore more comprehensible to man. Torah laws are made by Hashem – [they are thus] loftier, more distant, transcendent, [and] less comprehensible to man. Rashi presents a progression of concepts that are increasingly difficult for man to grasp.[3] "My commandments" he explains as logical rules in the Torah, that, had they not been written, ought to have been commanded. This is the part of the transcendent Torah that is most comprehensible to man, like theft and murder. "My decrees" he explains, as is the usual understanding, the illogical, seemingly arbitrary rules that the King decrees upon his servants, like the prohibitions to eat pork or wear *sha'atnez*. These are written but incomprehensible, and the evil inclination and the nations of the world challenge us with them. "My teaching [Torah]" Rashi explains as the oral Torah given to Moshe on Sinai, the least comprehensible, for not only is it transcendent, it is not even written.

Ramban attacks Rashi's explanation for assuming that the patriarchs kept the Torah before it was given. How, then did Yaakov marry sisters? This is explicitly forbidden in the Torah [Lev. 18:18]. Ramban answers that the patriarchs learned the entire Torah through the Holy Spirit of prophecy, and kept it as one who does a thing without it having been commanded.[4] However, they kept it only in the Land of Israel,[5] for the Torah is "the judgment

---

3. Be'er Hagola 17a: A counter-intuitive law is brought in Eruvin 21b – he who transgresses the laws of the rabbis is guilty of a capital offence. This is because their decrees were befitting their wisdom. Man operates according to the laws of nature – if he comes too close to fire, he will immediately suffer a burn. If he sins against Hashem, his punishment will be slower to come. When he sins against the decrees of the rabbis, which are human *sechel*, his punishment comes immediately in this world, but when he transgresses the laws of the Torah, which are Godly, his punishment is generally deferred to the World to Come.

4. See Kid. 31a and Gur Arye 39:9[6].

5. 1:1[2]{12}

of the God of the Land" [Kings II, 17:26], which means it applies in the Land of Israel and not outside it. Yaakov married sisters in Padan Aram, and Amram married his aunt in Egypt [Ex. 6:20]. Ramban proceeds to give a different rendition of this verse.[6]

The midrash [BR 80:11] holds that the twelve sons of Yaakov did not marry Canaanite women, such that "Shaul the son of the Canaanite woman" [46:10] who went down to Egypt was the son of Dina by Shimon. If so, Dina married Shimon her brother. Furthermore, after Yosef disappears, Yaakov's "daughters" [37:35] comfort him, and Rashi notes Rabbi Yehuda's view that the twelve sons had twin sisters whom they married, along with Rabbi Nechemia's view that they married Canaanite women. How can we account for these incestuous marriages? One answer is that the patriarchs were considered converts, who are like newborns [Yeb. 22a] [and] not related to their siblings according to Torah law. They kept the Torah, but the forbidden sexual unions did not pertain to them! This answers Ramban's objection while preserving Rashi's contention that the patriarchs kept all the commandments.

An even better answer to Ramban's objection derives from an analysis of doing something not commanded. Consider a woman who is not required to fulfill time-bound positive commandments [Kid. 29a], or a blind man according to Rabbi Yehuda [B.K. 87a], who receives reward for deeds not commanded, even though it is a lesser reward than she or he would have received had they been commanded. But the reward is limited to positive commandments.[7] Furthermore, one who fasts is called a sinner,

---

6. Ramban, ad loc.: "My safeguards" refers to belief in God…keeping Him in one's heart and calling in the name of Hashem, in order to return the multitudes to His service. "My commandments" refers to "Go out of your land," the driving out of the maidservant and her son, and the binding of Yitzchak. "My decrees" refers to walking in His ways, imitating Him in kindness and mercy, doing righteousness and justice, and commanding his children to do the same. "My Torah" refers to *mila* and the laws of the sons of Noach.

7. Kid.39a: The only case in which abstaining from a negative commandment is rewarded is if the prohibited act falls into his hand and he is 'saved.' See

as is a *nazir,* who denies himself just wine and must bring a sin offering [Ta'an. 11a]![8] Therefore, the patriarchs would have been in error had they observed the negative precepts without having been commanded! This is how Yaakov could marry sisters and his sons their own sisters.[9]

MDK: Accepting Rashi's contention that the commandments of the Torah pertained to the patriarchs, Gur Arye is faced with the apparent blatant violation of the incest laws by Yaakov, Shimon, and according to Rabbi Yehuda, the rest of the brothers who married their twin sisters. He gives two answers when the matter is discussed in Parashat Vayigash. The first, unsupported by a textual source, avers a requirement for conversion for all until the giving of the Torah. The newly converted are considered newborn without family, and incest does not apply. The second argues that the patriarch's observance was limited to positive commandments, for self-denial when not commanded is, according to Rambam, forbidden. It is clear one must be circumspect about stringencies [chumrot].

    Tiferet Yisrael 20:61a, Derech Hachaim 2:1, 67a, Chidushei Agadot on Kid. 39b, 2:140b and on Hul. 91a, 4:105a. Rabbenu Yona, Sha'arei Teshuva 9:3 and Rambam, Perush Hamishnayot, Ab. 2:1 disagree.

8. Derech Hachaim 2:13, 105a: "Do not be wicked before yourself" means do not act badly even toward yourself, to deny yourself something unnecessarily. The same way one who is kind to himself is called saintly [Prov. 11:17], one who acts badly toward himself is called wicked. Netiv Hateshuva 7, 2:167b: He who commits suicide is guilty of a sin deserving of capital punishment. If he torments himself, he is similarly guilty [on a different scale]. Rambam, Laws of Character Traits 5:1: One should not refrain from doing that which the Torah does not proscribe. Yer. Ned. 9:1: Is all the Torah prohibits not enough for you? You seek to prohibit additional things upon yourself! For opposing view, see Rashi, Lev. 19:2.

9. Gur Arye 46:10[5].

WHY YITZCHAK LOVED ESAV

27:21. And Yitzchak said to Yaakov: Please approach that I might feel you...

Rashi: He said to himself, "Esav doesn't usually refer to Hashem in his speech, and this one just said 'Hashem, your God, arranged it for me.'"

Gur Arye: Yitzchak and Esav had something in common – neither referred to Hashem in his speech. Yitzchak gave Esav the benefit of the doubt[10] and thought the reason for this was Esav's care not to use Hashem's name in vain. If a person serves Hashem out of fear, he will not mention His name, out of fright.[11] Yitzchak had this attribute, as it is written, "the Dread of Yitzchak was with me" [31:42].[12] Fear of Hashem was his great attribute. He loved Esav, who, he perceived, was like him in this respect.[13] As for Yaakov, who did mention His name, Yitzchak held that he served Hashem out of love, and a lover mentions his beloved continually, as the beloved is always on his mind.[14] Yitzchak gave his soul over to

---

10. Shebu. 30a: Judge your fellow man toward the side of innocence – this is a corollary of "in righteousness shall you judge your fellow man" [Lev. 19:15].

11. See Derech Hachaim 1:3, 32b, Netiv Yirat Hashem 3:2, 29a, and Pachad Yitzchak, Shab. 2:2. Derasha Leshabbat Shuva 67b: He who mentions Hashem's name in vain does not fear heaven at all. If he did, it would be as if, uninvited, he entered the palace of a king of flesh and blood – that would be rebellion, and he would not do it. Hashem's name is not an ordinary name – with two letters of it He created everything [Rashi, 2:4]. Mentioning His name is removing the yoke and the awe of the Holy One, blessed be He.

12. See Netiv Hateshuva 2:2, 152b and Netiv Habusha 1:2, 200a.

13. See Zohar 1:137b.

14. Rambam, Laws of Ethics 6:3: We are commanded to love every person of Israel like ourselves. This means we must speak in praise of each of them. Laws of Foundations of Torah 2:2: The moment a person understands His deeds and His great and wondrous creations, and sees in them boundless wisdom, he loves, praises, and glorifies Hashem.

Hashem and negated himself in his relationship with Hashem – there was no separation between him and Hashem.[15] This is how Yitzchak, who never mentioned Hashem's name, identified with Esav.

If one has the fear of Heaven, he cleaves completely to Him. Love of Heaven is not the same; it is more of a balanced relationship – a connection between beloveds. With awe, a person negates his existence with respect to Hashem…and has no *kiyum* [fulfilment, ongoing existence] except in Him.[16]

MDK: Gur Arye, later in Parashat Va'era, presents a beautiful geometric analogy describing the relationship of the patriarchs. Consider three dots in a row –

*   *   *

On the left is Avraham, whose characteristic was Kindness. He loved Hashem boundlessly and loved people to a fault. He prayed for Avimelech and pleaded for Sedom and Yishmael. He brought ethics and monotheism to the world, but only one of his nine sons (Yishmael, Yitzchak and seven sons of Ketura) was fit to carry on his legacy.

On the right is Yitzchak, who, having experienced the Akeda, *was in a perpetual state of extreme Awe of Hashem, which he perfected, but at a cost. Only one of his two sons was fit to carry on the legacy.*

In the middle is Yaakov, the bechir sheba'avot [*choicest of the patriarchs*] *who learned and was nourished from his father and his grandfather and integrated Kindness and Awe into his characteristic,* Tiferet, Splendor. *His bed was complete – all twelve of his sons were fit to carry on the legacy.*

---

15. Netzach Yisrael 13, 78a.
16. Tiferet Yisrael 10:35b.

ESAV'S BLESSING

27:37: And Yitzchak answered and said to Esav:
Behold I have made him a lord over you...

Rashi: This is the seventh blessing given Yaakov, yet he mentions it first here. He said to Esav, "What use are blessings to you? If you acquire possessions, they are his, for I have made him a lord over you, and whatever a servant acquires, his master acquires."

Gur Arye: According to Rashi's account, why does Esav answer, "Do you have but one blessing, my father?" [27:38]. Yitzchak had just said there was no purpose to further blessings! The answer is, Esav meant, "Is there a blessing you can give me that Yaakov can not lay claim to?" So Yitzchak blessed him with "the fat of the earth shall be your dwelling..." [27:39],[17] which does not apply to the sons of Israel, for the Holy Land belongs to them, and they do not desire an impure land.[18] "...You shall live by your sword..." [27:40] is likewise beyond the bounds of Yaakov's blessing, as it is the opposite of Yaakov's attributes of *shalom*[19] and truth.[20] Thus the blessings Esav received did not belong to Yaakov.

---

17. Rashi 27:39: This is the Italian province of Greece.
18. Shab. 15a: The rabbis decreed ritual impurity on the lands of the other nations. Gevurot Hashem 8:46a: The Land belongs to Israel – both have transcendent status. See Netiv Ha'avoda 18:1, 140b.
19. Zohar 3:12: "He makes *shalom* in His high places" [Job 25:2] – This refers to Yaakov, who makes *shalom* through his attachment to Avraham and Yitzchak. Sword and *shalom* are opposites, as in Lev. 26:6: I have placed *shalom* on the land...and no sword shall pass through your land.
20. Mic. 7:20: Attribute truth to Yaakov. Netzach Yisrael 4:21b: Yaakov is the opposite of bloodshed, for he is life, as it says, "Yaakov our father did not die" [Ta'an. 5b]. Esav was red, a sign he would be a murderer [Rashi 25:25]. Additionally, Yaakov never saw a seminal emission [Rashi 49:3], which is considered a little like bloodshed, since it is possible a person could be created from it.

RIVKA'S SPECIAL GIFT

28:5. And Yitzchak sent Yaakov who went to Padan Aram, to Lavan the son of Betuel the Aramean, the brother of Rivka, the mother of Yaakov and Esav.

Rashi: I don't know what "the mother of Yaakov and Esav" [a seemingly redundant description of Rivka] comes to teach us.

Gur Arye: Yitzchak understood that one of his offspring needed to be free of defect in his offspring, to have a "completed bed" [Torat Kohanim, Lev. 26:42].[21] Consider that Avraham's trait was kindness, and contrariwise, Yitzchak's trait was justice, and both of these greats produced defective offspring. Yaakov steered the middle course – his trait was truth, for truth does not incline to left or right. Yitzchak knew Yaakov would incorporate his own trait with those of his father and grandfather, and the result would be a "complete bed." Rivka was the one who first experienced during her pregnancy the struggle of the opposing forces of her twins, and was able to differentiate the fine from the dross. Yitzchak conceded that Rivka and, by extension, her family, could remove that which was defective and extract the purified product. This was the hope of Yitzchak – that Yaakov would marry Lavan's daughters and produce the blessed, purified seed. The description of Rivka as "mother of Yaakov and Esav" teaches us that by recognizing the evil nature of her son Esav, she purified the Jewish People. This family trait would aid in its survival.

Also, "the mother of Yaakov and Esav" is a reference to the "two nations" [25:23] in her womb – the house of Betuel is capable

---

21. Gevurot Hashem 9:58b.

of producing nations. For these reasons, Lavan was fit to be, in spite of his wickedness, a grandfather of the nation of Israel.[22]

MDK: There are many instances where Rashi fails to comment on a verse leaving us bereft of his understanding. When this happens, the supercommentaries are silent as well. This is one of those rare instances where Rashi tells us he fails to understand a verse. Yet here, Gur Arye offers solutions, that the antidote to Lavan's evil is also in his genetic heritage – the knowledge of how to identify that evil, to isolate and neutralize it. This is the gift of Rivka that Yitzchak is now able to acknowledge, and that Yaakov must seek in his mates. Perhaps he saw that Israel would need toughness to survive.

---

22. Gevurot Hashem 54:237: Lavan the Aramite was Yaakov's opposite, and because of this, he wanted to destroy all. Also 5:35b: An opposite can come out of its opposite, and this is even more likely if the opposites are more distant from one another. This explains Avraham coming from Terach, and Chizkiahu from Achaz. This is the reason for Avraham's sojourn in Ur Kasdim and Israel's sojourn in Egypt

Vayetze

THE IMPACT OF A RIGHTEOUS PERSON ON A PLACE

28:10. And Yaakov departed Be'er Sheva and went to Charan.

Rashi: It need only to have written, "And Yaakov went to Charan." Why mention his departure? It tells us that when a righteous person leaves a place, it makes an impression. For while he is in a city, he is its magnificence, its radiance, its glory. When he departs from there, its magnificence has gone away, its radiance has gone away, its glory has gone away. Similarly, "And she departed from the place" [Ruth 1:7].

Gur Arye: These three things are mentioned because a righteous person in a city guides its residents in the fear of heaven, which means the commandments of Hashem – this is the city's magnificence. Second, he imparts wisdom – this is its radiance. Third, he teaches them good and proper character traits, like those found in the tractate, *Avot*[1] – that is the city's glory.

"Magnificence" [*hod*] is an expression of praise, as in "*Hodu lashem*" [Ps. 136:1], which means "Praise Hashem," applied to one

---

1.   Derech Hachaim, Intro. 8a: The most precious and praiseworthy tractate is Avot. If a person wishes to be saintly, he should fulfill the words of Avot. The main principle of saintliness [*chasidut*] is achieving harmonious perfection within himself. This *shelemut* is good character.

who fears heaven, as in "a woman who fears Hashem is praised" [Prov. 31:30].[2] Here it means the one who teaches people Hashem's commandments.

Corresponding to the wisdom he imparts to them, "radiance" departs when he departs. Wisdom is radiance, as the Talmud says [Shab. 156a] that if one is born on Wednesday, he will be a wise man and a luminary [n'hir], which Rashi defines as a "man of radiance [ziv]."[3] Similarly, "The wisdom of a man will illuminate his face" [Eccl. 8:1].

"Glory [hadar] departs from the city" refers to his praiseworthy character traits, which are glorious,[4] and set an example for all to emulate.

MDK: Gur Arye seems to play fast and loose with definitions in this selection. However, the novel juxtaposition of the "woman of valor" to Rashi's interpretation adds meaning and texture to the verse.

---

2. Maharal, Derasha al Hatorah 32a: There are three levels: one who behaves courteously so as to bear grace [chen] in the eyes of all, another whose wisdom is beauty [yofi] which is called light, and another who fears Hashem; this one is most praiseworthy. Netiv Yirat Hashem 3:2, 26a: To make known the high level of the fear of heaven, Shlomo said, "Grace is deceitful and beauty is vain, a woman who fears Hashem is to be praised" [Prov. 31:30].

3. See Tiferet Yisrael 46:143a, Derech Hachaim 6:3, 287a, and Gur Arye 10:29[38] {81}. Hashem created the luminaries on Wednesday, thus Wednesday's child will be a luminary, i.e., a wise person.

4. Rashi, Ex. 23:3: "You shall not tehedar [honor, favor] a poor man in his dispute," means not to single him out for deference.

THE PLACE

28:11. And he encountered *the* place and spent
the night there…

Rashi: It doesn't say which place, but the place *implies a place mentioned elsewhere. This is Mount Moria, about which it is said, "and
he saw* the place *from afar" [22:4].*

Gur Arye: Maybe the place is Chevron, which is geographically
closer, as well as textually [23:19], than Mount Moria [22:4]. But
the *patach* [vowel sound 'a'] in *bamakom* connotes the definite
article "the" and must refer to a specific, known place mentioned
in the Torah, the fitting place for the revelation of the Divine
Presence [*Shechina*].[5] The only place so specified is the place
to which Avraham was commanded to bring his only son for a
sacrifice, *the* place he saw from afar [22:4], *the* place Hashem
will choose to place His Name [Deut. 12:11], *the* place Yaakov
encountered.

 Makom [place, Omnipresent] has another special meaning –
sustainer of one who stands in it [*mekayem*].[6] This clearly applies
to the Holy Temple, which is an essential feature of the world. Just
as all the organs of the body get their life force from the heart, the
entire world drinks of the extract of the Land of Israel, and the
Holy Temple is the main essence of the Land of Israel.[7]

MDK: The oral component of the Masoretic text (as well as the

---

5. Deut. 12:11: *The* place where Hashem, your God, will choose to place His
 Name, there you will bring all that I will command you [the sacrifices]….
 Gur Arye, Ex. 21:1[3]: Sacrifice [*korban*] means, and contains the same letters
 as, closeness [*hitkarvut*] to Hashem. See Chidushei Agadot on Shebu. 9a, 215b
 and Derasha Leshabbat Hagadol 215b.
6. Or Chadash 154b.
7. Derech Hachaim 5:20,270b.

written component) is considered halacha leMoshe miSinai, *oral transmission of Torah direct from Hashem [Ned. 37b], and is thus a matter worthy of interpretation. Here the pronunciation of a single letter gives rise to the midrash that explains the verse.*

YAAKOV'S VOW – IS IT REALLY A PLEA?

28:20–21. And Yaakov took a vow, saying, "If Hashem will be with me, and guard me on this way.... I will return to my father's house and Hashem will be a God to me."

Rashi: The last statement, "Hashem will be a God to me," means that His Name will prevail upon me from beginning to end, that no defect will be found in my progeny...

Gur Arye: Rashi means that one ought to be careful not to interpret the verse to mean, Heaven forbid, that Yaakov's acceptance of Hashem is contingent on the fulfillment of his prayer! Rather it is an additional prayer that "He prevail upon me" to ensure the purity of his progeny.

MDK: The verses could be read as an arrogant challenge to Hashem – deliver me safely if You want me to continue to relate to You as my God. Instead, it is a prayer – may Hashem prevail upon me that my actions result in the merit of my children.

WHY POVERTY IS LIKE DEATH

29:12. And Yaakov kissed Rachel, and he raised
his voice and cried.

*Rashi: He cried, for he foresaw with the Holy Spirit that she would
not be buried with him. Alternatively, he cried because his hands
were empty, not like those of his grandfather's servant, Eliezer, who
had nose rings, bracelets, and delicacies when he came to this place.
Elifaz, the son of Esav, pursued him at Esav's command to kill him,
and overtook him. Since Elifaz had grown up in Yitzchak's close
embrace, he withdrew his hand and refrained from killing his uncle,
whereupon he asked, "What shall I do to fulfill my father's command?" Yaakov said, "Take all I have, for the poor man is considered like a dead man."*

Gur Arye: Why is a poor man like a dead man? He does not make
a "living" [*chiyut*] on his own, while the living sustain themselves
and do not require the help of others. Since a poor man does not
sustain himself, he is not considered among the living.[8] Furthermore, we are commanded to sustain him [B.M. 88b], as it is written, "your brother shall live [be sustained] with you" [Lev. 25:36].[9]
Similarly, "He who dislikes gifts shall live" [Prov. 15:27] means he
who disdains living off others has his own *chiyut*.[10] *Chiyut* implies
self-sustaining life, and that is why the wellspring that flows on its

---

8. See Gur Arye, Ex. 4:19: *Chiyut* is the acceptance of the blessing from above
   that does not stop, called life. Something that ceases is death, while something unceasing is life. When a person is impoverished and his blessing ceases,
   he is considered dead. Also see Netiv Hatorah 4, 1:20b and Netiv Haosher 1,
   2:224a.
9. Netiv Yirat Hashem 3, 2:29b: Sustenance is the *chiyut* [life, livelihood] of a
   person.
10. Netiv Haosher 1, 2:223b and Netiv Hatorah 4, 1:20b.

own and receives no water from another source is called "living wellspring" or "wellspring of life" [s.o.s. 4:15].

MDK: It is intriguing that the purport of this derashah *is found in the colloquial expression in English and other languages for sustenance – "to make a living."*

RACHEL'S ENVY

30:1. And Rachel saw that she had not borne children to Yaakov, and she became envious of her sister; she said to Yaakov, "Give me children – if not, I am dead."

Rashi: She envied her sister's good deeds, saying, "She must be more righteous than I, or else she would not be worthy of children."

Her demand, that her husband give her children, was by way of admonishing him – "Is this the way your father acted toward your mother? Did he not pray for her?"

Rachel considered childlessness tantamount to death. From here we see that a childless person is considered as if dead.

Gur Arye: The midrash quoted by Rashi [BR 71:6] changes the apparent target of Rachel's envy from Leah or her good fortune to her righteousness. In an effort to better herself, Rachel looked to her sister's deeds. It would be unseemly and incompatible with her character for Rachel to be jealous of her sister, God forbid. The rabbis say, "Envy removes a person from the world" [Ab. 4:22].

"Give me children" cannot be taken literally, for Yaakov did not have the fulfillment of that request within his power. Rather, she asked of him something he could do – pray to Hashem to allow her to conceive and bear children as his father Yitzchak had done for his mother Rivka.

Why is childlessness tantamount to death? Because life is unceasing, as in "a well of living waters" [S.O.S. 4:15].[11] Its source flows continuously, whereas death is loss and cessation.[12] A person who leaves no offspring has an interruption of his *toldot* [offspring,

---

11. See 11:32[20] and 32:12[18] and Chidushei Agadot on R.H. 16b, 1:109b.
12. 49:33[24] and Or Chadash 220a.

history], therefore he is considered as dead.[13] The live person is like the well, called "life which continues to flow," like one who has produced offspring has such a flowing source.[14]

MDK: This is an example of the rabbis departing from the simple understanding of the text in order to avoid the picture of an unfettered emotional outburst in the saintly matriarch.

---

13. See Netiv Hayisurin 2, 2:176b. Chidushei Agadot on Ned. 64b, 2:23a: He who has no children to reproduce his mold and form does not himself have mold and form. The idea of a mold is to reproduce. Chidushei Agadot on Yeb. 64a, 1:141a: That which does not stop is called "life," for one who is involved in the process of reproduction is alive, as he cleaves to the uninterrupted source by having offspring. If one eschews the process of reproduction, he removes himself from the wellspring of life...

14. Gevurot Hashem 71:326a: The heart is the honored organ that contains the life force [*chiyut*], and from it the other organs receive their life force. The part of the tree that reawakens the potential to grow fruit is called *livluv* [bud] from *lev* [heart]. A tree that buds is realizing the potential to bring forth its life force. Thus a person who fails to reproduce and bring forth fruit is considered as dead. Chidushei Agadot on Yeb. 64a, 1:141a: You must also know and understand that he who partakes of the commandment to be fruitful and multiply is considered a community person, for reproduction establishes the community and stabilizes it, and those who do it are considered alive. On the other hand, those who do not reproduce are obliged to die for excluding themselves from the community and their part in sustaining it.

A DOMESTIC SQUABBLE

> 30:2. Yaakov's anger flared at Rachel and he said,
> "Am I instead of God who has withheld from you
> the fruit of the womb?"

Rashi: You say I should act like my father, but I am not like my father. He did not have children, but I do. Hashem has withheld children from you, not from me.

Gur Arye: The midrash cited by Rashi [BR 71:19] places Rachel's demand in the context of asking him to pray for her. Ramban wonders, why should Yaakov have been angered by that? Don't the righteous pray for others? Consider Eliahu [Kings I 18:21] and Elisha [Kings II 4:33] who prayed on behalf of strange women. Ramban answers that Yaakov was insensitive and behaved badly toward his distraught wife, and for this Hashem berated him, saying, "Is this a way to answer a woman afflicted by barrenness? I swear! Your children are destined to stand before her son Yosef" [BR 71:10].

However, Yaakov may have been justified. The patriarchs are the foundation of the world [Gur Arye 32:3[2]], and the "tribes," Yaakov's twelve sons, are the main spiritual essence of the world, each of whom is the main reason for creation. These children are not like other children, and Hashem intended who the mother of each should be.[15] Yaakov did not wish to alter the matter by praying, unlike his father who knew all his progeny would be from his only soul mate, Rivka.[16]

MDK: Ramban, as is his way, does not refrain from chiding our heroes, perhaps that we might learn from their mistakes. For example,

---

15. See 48:7[12].
16. 25:26[40]: Once Yitzchak saw all the miracles done for Eliezer, he reached the conclusion that this mate and no other was from Hashem.

when Avram finds famine in Kenaan, Ramban says he should have stayed and not lacked faith that Hashem would take care of him. Furthermore, he put Sarai at risk of rape or worse. For this, says Ramban, Egyptian exile was decreed upon the Jewish people. Here, Ramban's derashah accuses Yaakov of insensitivity. Maharal, as is his way, comes to Yaakov's and Rashi's defense.

AVRAHAM MUST HAVE PRAYED FOR SARA – HASHEM DOES NOT GRANT SOMETHING NOT ASKED FOR

30:3. And she said, "Here is my maid Bilha – come to her, that she may bear upon my knees, and I too will be built up through her."

Rashi: What is meant by "too"? She said to him, "Your grandfather, Avraham, had offspring by Hagar, yet he girded his loins, redoubling his effort to pray on Sara's behalf." He replied, "My grandmother brought a rival wife into her house." She said to him, "If this is what is preventing my bearing children, here is my maid Bilha..., and I too may be built up, like Sara" [BR 71:7].

Gur Arye: All this is predicated on the notion that Avraham prayed for Sara, but we have no text to corroborate that! We can infer for certain that he prayed for her, since Hashem promised she would bear a son [17:19], and such a promise would not be given without Avraham praying for it, for something not asked for is not given.[17]

The rabbis relate [Tanchuma, Re'e 8] that the Land of Israel is called "the desired land" [Jer. 3:9] because the patriarchs desired it. Avraham wanted it, as he said, "How will I know I will inherit it?" [15:8]. Yitzchak wanted it as Hashem said to him, "Live in this land and I will be with you and bless you, for I will give all these lands to you and your progeny" [26:3]. How does the latter verse prove that Yitzchak wanted the Land of Israel? The answer is, if he hadn't prayed for it, Hashem would not have promised it. Hashem's promise implies and assumes Yitzchak's prayer.

Avraham prayed for Sara, because a righteous person always

---

17. Ramban, Ex. 4:10: Because of his desire not to go to Paro, Moshe did not ask Hashem to cure his heaviness of tongue, so Hashem did not heal him.

prays for that which he thinks he lacks.[18] What he desires becomes his prayer, for "He does the will of those who fear Him" [Ps. 155:19]. Rachel's complaint was that Avraham wanted Sara to conceive and he prayed for it, while Yaakov appeared to lack the desire that Rachel conceive.

MDK: Gur Arye takes the missing link in Rachel's argument and makes it an implicit imperative. We are first introduced to the notion of the requirement to pray in order that something happen in Rashi, Genesis [2:5]: "Hashem had not brought rain to the earth, for there was no man to pray for it." Although Maharal's logic can be faulted – he derives a lesson from a text that does not exist – the lesson is still beautiful.

---

18. See Chidushei Agadot on Yeb. 64a, 2:141b.

YOSEF'S FLAME EMERGES FROM YAAKOV'S FIRE

30:25. And it was when Rachel bore Yosef, Yaakov
said to Lavan, "Send me away...."

Rashi: Yosef was the foil of Esav, as the prophet said [Ob. 1:18], "The House of Yaakov shall be fire, and the House of Yosef, flame, and the House of Esav, straw." Fire without flame cannot rule over a wide distance. When Yosef was born, Yaakov gained confidence in Hashem's protection and wished to return.

Gur Arye: Esav and Yaakov opposed each other in everything, and Yosef was Yaakov's main offspring, as it is written, "These are the children of Yaakov, Yosef..." [Rashi 37:2]. Just as flame emerges from fire, Yosef emerges from Yaakov [B.K. 59:2]. Having shared the womb, Yaakov was too close to Esav to have power over him. Children actuate the potential of parents,[19] and now Yaakov had attained *shelemut*. The fire is the potential and the flame is its actuation. This is why Moshe chose Yehoshua, a descendant of Yosef, to lead the army that confronted Amalek, descendants of Esav [Ex. 18:12]. The Holy Zohar tells us [3:215a] that the planet Mars is united with Esav and that [1:200b] the constellation of Yosef is Taurus.[20] When Mars occurs in conjunction with Taurus,[21] its power is weakened. Thus Yosef is the foil of Esav.

---

19. See 28:11[17]. Gur Arye 38:15[9]: Children are like *tzitzit* [ritual fringes] that break forth from a person's clothing, so, too, children break forth from his or her body. Netiv Ha'avoda 15, 1:123b: The commandment of *tzitzit* expresses the actualization of man's potential. *Tzitzit* connotes *"tzitz hasade"* [sprouting forth of the field] [Isa. 40:6], the emergence of the plant from the earth.

20. 49:22.

21. Taurus contains a weak red star. See Netzach Yisrael 17, 93a; Be'er Hagola 6:116b; Or Chadash 51a; and Gevurot Hashem 47:187b.

TWO BANDS OF ANGELS

32:1. And Yaakov went on his way, and angels of
God came to meet him.

Rashi: Angels of the Land of Israel came to meet him to accompany him to the Land.

Gur Arye: Rashi draws on the midrash [BR 74:17 and Tanchuma, Vayishlach 3]. Ramban finds this difficult, for he was still far from the Land of Israel, as the Land is not mentioned till "and Yaakov came complete to the city of Shechem which is in the Land of Kenaan" [33:18]. In my opinion, there is no difficulty, for he was in the process of going to the Land and the angels of the Land came to protect him on the way, as there was a need for him in the Land of Israel. These angels were there to guarantee that nothing should hold him back from coming to the Land, while the angels of outside the Land were still there to protect him from any other danger. If so, why didn't the angels come at Yaakov's departure from Charan? The answer is that till Hashem warned Lavan [31:24], Yaakov's departure was in jeopardy. Once Lavan and Yaakov separated in peace, it became clear that Yaakov was truly en route to the Land and the angels came.

Rashi on the next verse [32:2] explains the name given Yaakov's next stop, *Machanaim* [encampments], as referring to the camps of the two groups of angels, those of the Land of Israel and those of outside the Land. Consider the parallel event – Yaakov's ladder dream [28:12], on which Rashi notes that first the angels of the Land of Israel ascended, then the angel of outside the Land descended. The moment Yaakov was left unaccompanied and unprotected, Hashem stood over him. At Machanaim there was a need for both groups of angels to protect him, as explained above.

Now let us examine the asymmetries between the two events. Why did the outside angels not accompany Yaakov when he began his journey from Be'er Sheva? The answer is, when he left the

Land, it was not because of the attraction of another land, but rather in order to save his life [Rashi 29:13]. To descend from the Land, he did not need extra protection, but his ascent [*aliya*] to the Land of Israel[22] occasioned the accompaniment of the angels of the Land.

Why did those same angels depart from Yaakov, ascending the ladder before he actually left the Land? Yerushalayim[23] is nowhere near the border. The answer is found in a *Mishna* in Ketubot [110b]: "All go up to Yerushalayim, but all do not go down," which Rashi explains, "A person may force his entire family to go up to Yerushalayim to live with him, but he may not force them to leave Yerushalayim against their will." Then Yaakov left Mount Moriah [Rashi 28:17], which is Yerushalayim [Rashi 22:2], and this is tantamount to leaving the Land of Israel completely, for Yerushalayim is holier than the rest of the Land [Kaylim 1:8]. As he left there, the angels of the Land of Israel ascended. May Hashem bestow merit on us by bringing us up to that place, to see it built, in all its glory.

MDK: Gur Arye tends to finish each parasha on a homiletic note. This sounds a little like a Shabbat sermon.

---

22. Be'er Hagola 6, 131b and Chidushei Agadot on Ket. 110b, 1:164 from Tanchuma, Kedoshim 10: The Land of Israel is the center of the world and Yerushalayim is the center of the Land of Israel. Chidushei Agadot on R.H. 23a, 1:125b: Yerushalayim is the essence and the heart of the Land of Israel, for everything depends on it. Netiv Ha'avoda 18, 1:136b: The Land is not just the harmonious perfection of nature, it is the harmonious perfection of Godly spirituality, and it is known that the atmosphere of the Land of Israel makes one wise [B.B. 158b]...there is nothing as completely Godly as Yerushalayim and the Holy Temple.

23. See Rashi 28:17.

Vayishlach

YAAKOV'S TWIN FEARS

32:7–8. "…He [Esav] is heading toward you, and four hundred men are with him." And Yaakov became very frightened, and it distressed him…

Rashi: "He was frightened" that he would be killed, "and it distressed him" that he might kill others.

Gur Arye: Superficially, fright and distress seem similar. Rashi's midrash [BR 76:2, Tanchuma, Vayishlach 4] attributes the two to separate concerns. The fright was simple fear for his life. The distress stemmed from the possibility that if Esav tried to kill him, he would be obliged to preemptively kill Esav first, as the sages dictate [Sanh.72a]: "If one comes to kill, kill him first." Yaakov's concern was his father Yitzchak's reaction to this – loving Esav, his father might come to curse his killer.

There is a problem with this interpretation – the midrash is careful to pluralize the object of Yaakov's potential killing, with the word "others." It could not mean Esav alone. Could it mean Esav's four hundred men? If they came to kill, Yaakov could kill them with impunity. But what if they were pressed into duty against their will? Even then, they could be preemptively killed under the doctrine [Pes. 25a]: Any sin in the Torah may be committed to save one's life except three – idolatry, adultery, and murder – which means if someone said, "kill this man or I will kill you," the subject of the command must die rather than kill. The *Gemara* goes on to state the reason – who's to say your blood is redder than his? Perhaps his blood is redder than yours! Thus, Esav's men could not resort to a "just carrying out orders" defense, and should they intend to kill Yaakov, he would clearly be justified in preempting them. Why, then, should Yaakov be distressed? The answer lies in how the situation presents itself. Four hundred men march toward him and he does not know if they intend to kill him. If they did not intend to kill and he preemptively kills them, he could be held accountable for a kind of negligent manslaughter.[1] This is why he was distressed that he might kill others.

Why did he fear for his own life? Was he not promised [28:15], "Behold I am with you and will guard you…"? The *Gemara* answers [Ber. 4a, Sanh. 98b; cited by Rashi 32:10] that he feared the loss of the promise on account of sin. Does Hashem retract His word? In the case of prophecy, He does not, because fulfillment of prophecy depends solely on Him. A promise [*havtacha*] is a reward for righteousness, and thus dependent on the recipient of the promise.[2] This is why a prophecy is stated in the past tense, as Rashi says on [15:18], "to your seed I gave this land," that Hashem's statement virtually renders it a completed act.[3] On the other hand, a promise is made to the recipient as he is at the time of the promise, and if he changes, the promise can change as well. Thus Yaakov feared some sin on his part might have voided Hashem's prior promise of protection.

---

1. Derech Hachaim 4:4, 167b: As a rule, a negligent act is not a serious sin, since it lacks will and intent. The Torah is more stringent in the negligent taking of a life since the outcome is so important. That is why the punishment for negligent homicide is exile [Num. 35:25]. Damages are also dealt with stringently, as it is said [B.K. 26a]: "A person is perpetually [responsible], whether [the act was committed] intentionally or unintentionally and negligent, willingly, or as a victim of happenstance, for in the end, he caused damage to another."
2. See Gevurot Hashem 7:40b, Ab. 5:16.
3. See Isa. 24:8.

MDK: Yaakov, the man of peace, was grappling with what would be termed in modern parlance the Rules of Engagement. Ethical dilemmas are always solved in the halachic context.

GUILE OR WISDOM?

34:13. And the sons of Yaakov answered Shechem and his father, Chamor, with *mirma* [guile, wisdom], and they spoke. This was on account of his having defiled their sister, Dina.

Rashi: The last part of the verse is related by the Torah's Author to justify their negotiation as wisdom rather than guile.

Gur Arye: Considering what they were about to negotiate, the last part of the verse was not what Yaakov's sons would have discussed with Shechem and Chamor. Why then mention Dina's defilement? In order to redefine the meaning of *mirma* as "wisdom," or better, justified guile, the Author inserts the last part of the verse.

The narrative begs a troublesome question. Given that Shechem sinned and deserved his punishment, what was the sin of the entire city that necessitated its destruction? Rambam answers [Laws of Kings 9:14] that one of the seven commandments that apply to the sons of Noach is to have courts and carry out justice.[4] Transgression of any of the seven results in the death penalty [Sanh. 57a]. The community was aware of the abduction and rape of Dina by Shechem and did not bring him to justice.

I find this answer surprising. How could the prince of the land be brought to justice? They feared the ruling family. They could not be held accountable, for "in the case of coercion, the Torah absolves" [B.K. 28b].

The story must be viewed in an international context. The Torah refers to Israel and Shechem as separate nations, as it is written [34:16], "and we shall be one nation." The Torah permits the Jewish nation to wage war.[5] With respect to the caveat [Deut. 20:10],

---

4. Sanh. 56b: Just as Israel is commanded to set up courts in every principality, the sons of Noach are similarly commanded.

5. Deut. 20:1: When you go to war against your enemy...

"When you approach a city to wage war upon it, you shall offer them the option of surrender," this only applies in the absence of provocation.[6] Here they were provoked by an abominable act, and even though it was an act of only one of them, the Jewish nation was permitted to respond.[7] Shechem attacked Israel, and Israel, utilizing the sort of guile justified when one's nation is threatened, annihilated their enemy.

MDK: In the summer of 5766, two Israeli soldiers were kidnapped at the Lebanese border. Gur Arye would certainly justify the Israeli response.

---

6. See Sifri 20:10, Rambam, Laws of Kings 6:6, and Ramban, Deut. 2:34.
7. See Deut, 25:18 and Ex. 17:14–16 and Judges 19–20.

PLACES CAUSE EVENTS

> 35:13. And God arose from him in the place
> where He spoke to him.

Rashi: "In the place where He spoke to him" seems to serve no purpose. I do not know what it teaches us.

Gur Arye: It surprises me that Rashi does not get the message of the verse. The place where Hashem spoke to Yaakov, promising him nationhood and the Land, was the place set aside as the abode of the Divine Presence, which Yaakov had called El Bet El [35:7], which Rashi interprets to mean the revelation of the Divine Presence in Bet El. Nowhere else is a place named in Hashem's name on account of a revelation. The lesson to be learned is that the place is the causation of the revelation.

Places cause events [Sanh. 14b]. Avraham [12:6[12]] was shown Elon Moreh – plain of teaching – as the place for blessing [Mount Gerizim] and curse [Mount Eval]. While fighting the four kings, he pursued "as far as Dan" [14:14], where, as Rashi relates, his strength ebbed, for he saw that his children would establish a calf idol.[8] The *Gemara* states [Hor. 12b], "Kings are anointed only by springs in order that their reign be drawn out." This is not sorcery – many things are dependent on place. Springs are places designated for continuity, as the waters continue to flow. Thus the reign of the anointed king shall continue [Chidushei Agadot 4:59b].[9] Our verse is another example.

---

8. Chidushei Agadot on Sanh. 96a, 3:21a: Different places in the Land are specified for different purposes. Dan is most associated with idolatry in the way Yerushalayim has been prepared to be God's city.
9. Netzach Yisrael 28:136b: There is no doubt that there are places in the world designated as holy. The cave of Rabbi Shimon bar Yochai is such a place.

MDK: Makom [*Place, Omnipresent*] *is one of the names of God. Also, Ps. 90:2: My Lord, an abode have you been for us in all generations.*

THE THREE WHO ARE FORGIVEN

36:3. [Esav married] Bas'emat, the daughter of Yishmael...

Rashi: Elsewhere, she is called Machalat [28:9]. I found a midrash on the Book of Samuel that there are three whose sins are forgiven – one who converts, one who rises to high office, and one who marries. The reason is found here – when she married she became Machalat [forgiven], for her sins were forgiven.

Gur Arye: The reason for all three is that they are new human beings, and since it was the previous person who sinned, Hashem forgives them. The conclusion that they are new beings is reached differently for the three. In the case of marriage, before he or she was half a person and afterwards a whole person.[10] A prince who rises to high office – before, he was his individual personage, and now, so to speak, he "is" his entire people.[11] A convert is considered as a newborn [Yeb. 22a], a brand new creature.[12]

MDK: There is no superfluous letter in the Torah. It is intended that we learn from the most obscure verses regarding insignificant and unholy characters. Here are lessons we learn from Bas'emat's names which touch the lives of us all.

---

10. Yeb. 62b: A man is only half a man without a wife, as it is written, "male and female He created them and called their name Adam" [Gen. 5:2]. Zohar 3:83b: A son of man without a wife is a half body.
11. Rashi, Num. 21:21, on "and Yisrael sent": When the king sends, it is as if the whole nation sends. That is why, when the leader takes power, he is a new person, and his previous sins are forgiven. See also Chidushei Agadot on Yeb. 63b, 1:139a and on Sanh. 14a, 3:136a. 49:11[12]: The rider is like the king, for he rides his animal like a king rides his people. See also Chidushei Agadot on B.B. 3b, 3:57a; B.B. 4a, 3:58a; Sot. 10b, 2:42a; and Gevurot Hashem 14:71b.
12. See Gevurot Hashem 42:160a.

Book IV: The Sons of Yaakov

Vayeshev

THE CONSEQUENCE OF YOSEF'S PIETY

37:2. These are the offspring of Yaakov: Yosef at the age of seventeen was a shepherd with his brothers by the flock, and he was a youth with the sons of Bilha and Zilpa, his father's wives, and he would bring evil reports of them to their father.

Rashi: Any evil which he would see in his brothers, the sons of Lea, he would tell his father – that they would eat a limb from a living animal, that they would belittle the sons of the maidservants by calling them servants, and that they were suspect of sexual immorality. He was stricken for all three. For the report of eating a limb of a living animal, they slaughtered a goat when they sold him [37:13], but did not eat it live. For the report of having called their brothers servants, Yosef was sold as a slave [Ps. 105:17]. For the report of sexual immorality, his master's wife tried to seduce him [39:7].

Gur Arye: One could ask, as does Mizrachi, what it was that Yosef did wrong. There is a positive commandment to admonish one's fellow man to prevent sin [Lev. 19:17; Rambam, Laws of Ethics 6:7], and how better to accomplish this than to tell his father? As to the caveat that Hashem despises one who testifies singly when two witnesses are required, this would not apply here, since he only told his father, and his father would accept his testimony as if it

165

were from two witnesses [Pes. 113b].[1] From the *Gemara*, it seems Yosef would be required to tell his father. To report to his father was not evil – the content of the reports was evil.

The report was evil because the brothers did not do what Yosef thought they did. After properly slaughtering an animal, they cut a piece of meat from the incision site, salted it well, and then ate it. This is permitted, according to the *Gemara* [Hul. 33a][2] for the non-Jew as well as the Jew, based on the theory that nothing should be permitted for the Jew and forbidden for the non-Jew [Rashi, Hul. 121b]. Yosef reported the brothers had eaten meat from a live animal.

When the brothers called the sons of the maidservants, that is to say their father's wives who had been maidservants, the derogatory term, "servants," they didn't mean they were servants.[3] Yosef thought they considered them slaves.

When the brothers did business with the daughters of the local residents, Yosef thought this was forbidden on account of sexual immorality.[4]

How does the midrash know [BR 84:7] that the evil report [contained] these three things? The term *ra'a* [evil] is employed in the context of sexual immorality, as it is written [39:9], "How can I do this great *ra'a*?" With respect to servants, *ra'a* is mentioned [Ex. 21:8]: "And if she is *ra'a* in the eyes of her master…." When the messenger tells Yaakov [37:39], "An evil [*ra'a*] wild animal ate him," it implies he was eaten before he was killed, which hints at eating the limb of a living animal. All this explanation is found in Mizrachi.

---

1. See Netiv Hahochacha 1, 2:191b and Minchat Chinuch, Commandment 239:4.
2. Rambam, Laws of Slaughtering 1:2.
3. Kid. 28a: He who calls his friend "servant" must be excommunicated.
4. Kid. 81b: Shmuel holds it is forbidden to do business with females. Kid. 82a: Shmuel holds that if it is done for the sake of heaven, all [business] is permissible. Tosafot says there that we rely on the second opinion to permit business dealings with women.

The problem with Mizrachi's explanation of the midrash is that it is derived from a *gezera shavah* [a point of learning derived from the Torah usage of the same word in two contexts, suggesting the application of the characteristic of one to the other], and I did not learn this point of Torah from my teachers. The rule for *gezera shavah* is promulgated in the *Gemara* [Pes. 66a], indicating that a person cannot derive it on his own; rather it must be *kabala* [received wisdom] for it is subject to mischievous applications. It seems better to understand the verse through a close inspection of the words – "he was a shepherd with his brothers" would be understood without "by the flock." The redundancy refers to the "evil report" of transgressions relating to the flocks – the suspicion of eating the limb of a living animal. When the verse says, "the sons of Bilha and Zilpa," these, too, are the subjects of the "evil report," in that the brothers called them servants. From "the wives of his father" we have a reference to doing business with women, which relates to the issue of sexual immorality.

Mizrachi says the brothers were permitted to eat the meat of a slaughtered but still moving animal. Since ritual slaughter had not yet been taught, and the patriarchs kept the Torah on their own account,[5] not having been commanded it,[6] the Noachide prohibition of eating the meat of an animal before its death would be in place, notwithstanding ritual slaughter. If so, the question returns – what did Yosef do wrong to report it? Furthermore, the words of the midrash [BR 84:7] do not correspond to Mizrachi's version that the report was evil because the brothers had eaten of the live animal, as it says, "they were suspected," not that they ate.

Yosef reported suspicions that arose from his own stringencies. He was called "Yosef the Righteous" for a reason.[7] His

---

5. Yom. 28b: Avraham kept the whole Torah.
6. Ramban 26:5: It appears to me from the rabbis' account that Avraham, our father, learned the entire Torah through the Holy Spirit, and kept it as one who acts without having been commanded.
7. Tanchuma, Noach 5: Two people are called righteous, Noach and Yosef, as it is written [Amos 2:6]: "They sold the righteous one for money." Ket. 111a: Yosef

stringency regarding the limb of a live animal extended to not allowing his servants to cook for him.[8] He reported a suspicion of calling the sons of the maidservants "slaves" because the brothers distanced them. The brothers did not resist looking at the local girls, while the righteous one took care not to look at all, lest his evil inclination overtake him.[9] The brothers were not so careful in these three areas, while Yosef considered sin a serious matter, and distanced himself from it, even in a matter not forbidden.[10] In his state of piety, he was suspicious of any behavior he forbade himself. However, the brothers were not guilty of transgression.

The word *ra* [evil] is found in Scripture three times describing man's attributes – man's evil inclination, as in [8:21], "The inclination of the heart of man is evil from his youth"; the evil eye, as in [Deut. 15:9], "your eye will be evil toward your brother";[11] and the evil heart, as is found in many places.[12] Yosef was the completely

---

knew he was completely righteous. Zohar 1:189b: Yosef is called righteous, for he kept the holy covenant by resisting the non-Jewess.

8.   See Hul. 91a. and Git. 67b.

9.   Rambam, Laws of Forbidden Sexual Relations 1:24: The original saints and the greatest of sages…did not even consider the physical form of their wives. Shab. 53b: This person was so *tzanua* [private, modest] that he didn't know his wife was a hunchback till the day he died. B.B. 16a: Avraham did not look at even his own wife. See Netiv Haperishut, 2, 2: 114a-117b.

10. Be'er Hagola 1:18b: Rabbinical commandments are a separation from transgression that Hashem did not decree. Ibid. 15b: You see, the eyes have lids that they not suffer damage. The decrees of the sages are the defense of the Torah…The commandments need an extra guarding because the inclination of the heart of man is evil from his youth [8:21], and one must be concerned lest they be ruined. Therefore, they need fences and guards just like man's anatomic parts.

11. See Derech Hachaim 2:11, 99a; 21:14[16]<77,79>; and Derech Hachaim 2:14, 103b: A person who has the evil eye acts out the extra power of his soul to the degree that he can burn up everything with his eye. Also see Netiv Ayin Tov 1, 2:214–216.

12. Jer. 3:17: "they will no longer follow the visions of their evil heart," and Jer. 16:12: "Each one of you follows the vision of your evil heart." Netiv Lev Tov 1, 2:210b: Not to give the benefit of the doubt is the attribute of an "evil heart,"

righteous person, inasmuch as he is called Yosef the righteous, and he distanced himself from anything the Scripture called evil. What about the evil tongue [*lashon hara*]? Yosef would seem culpable of talebearing! The answer is the evil tongue is not found in Scripture[13] like the other three.

Consider that the three evils correspond to the three items in the report. The evil inclination is most clearly manifest in sexual immorality.[14] Calling the sons of the maidservants "servants" is a manifestation of the "evil eye" in the sense of denying them their appropriate status as brothers, equal sons of Yaakov. From this evil eye comes gratuitous hatred and jealousy that would deny status to one's fellow man.[15] The third evil, the evil heart, is cruelty to Hashem's creatures, such as eating the limb of a living animal.

Rabbi Yehoshua says [Ab. 2:11]: "The evil eye, the evil inclination, and the hatred of Hashem's creations remove a person from the world." The last is synonymous with the evil heart, for hatred is in the heart, as it is written [Lev. 19:17], "Do not hate your brother in your heart." It is fitting for such a person to be removed from the world, because Hashem, who created the world, created it as good, "and He saw that it was good" [1:4, etc.]. Existence is good, and evil negates it. Yosef thought he saw the three evils in his brothers. Nevertheless, Yosef sinned, as he should not have suspected them and reported to his father. We are commanded [Lev. 19:15], "in righteousness shall you judge your fellow man," which is interpreted by our sages [Shebu. 30a] to mean, judge all men on the side of merit.

Yosef was punished for the report measure for measure. For suspecting them of calling their brothers slaves, he was sold into

---

which is very bad…and brings out hatred of people. The same as the good-hearted person loves people, and wants good to happen to them, and gives them the benefit of the doubt; the evil-hearted person hates people.

13. It is in the Talmud, e.g., Yom. 48a: Incense atones for *lashon hara*.
14. Derech Hachaim 2:4, 103a: the essence of the evil inclination is sexual immorality, which applies to the body. See 6:11[22]<123>
15. Netiv Lev Tov 2:111b.

slavery. For suspecting them of sexual immorality, he was subjected to the temptations of Potifar's wife. For suspecting them of eating the limb of a living animal, he witnessed the proper slaughter of a goat, into whose blood his special coat was dipped.

PARENTAL FAVORITISM

37:3. Now Yisrael loved Yosef more than all his sons, and he made him a tunic of fine wool [*passim*].

Rashi: Aggadic midrash sees passim *as an acronym representing his troubles:* peh – Potifar, samech – socharim [*traders*], yud – Yishmaelim, mem – Midianim, *to each of whom he was sold.*

Gur Arye: The moral message of this midrash is that one should be careful to treat one's children without favoritism [Shab. 10b]. It was the minimal increment in the quality of Yosef's tunic over that of his brothers that "made" the troubles for his son. We learn this from the usage of "made" instead of "dressed."

The midrash implies that the merchants and the Midianites were two separate groups, while the verse [37:28] could be read as "Midianite merchants." There were presumably different groups within the caravan, and it is the way of merchants to trade with one another. If Potifar was Yosef's final owner, why mention him first? The answer is because the final outcome was in the inception of the thought.[16] Hashem wanted him to go down to Egypt and be Potifar's slave – that is why Potifar comes first.

MDK: Passim is variously rendered fine wool [Rashi], silk [Ibn Janach], royal [Ralbag], colorful [Radak], emroidered [Ibn Ezra], with pictures [Targum Yonatan], striped [Radak, Shorashim], or long [Baalei Tosafot, BR]. Rashi's midrash takes the word to be an acronym of the four parties that purchased Yosef, a fate that resulted from Yaakov's favoritism, embodied in the word passim.

---

16. Alkabetz, Lecha Dodi. Also see Gur Arye 1:1[7].

RULES OF DREAMS

> 37:10–11. And he had another dream and he told it to his brothers, and he said: "Behold, I dreamt another dream, and behold, the sun, the moon, and eleven stars were bowing to me." And he told his father and his brothers…

Rashi: After he told his brothers the dream, he told it to their father in their presence.

Gur Arye: Why did Yosef repeat the dream to the brothers? The sages have said [Ber. 55b] that all dreams follow the mouth, meaning the spoken interpretation.[17] The brothers had sarcastically dismissed the first dream, the sheaves dream, thinking it had no validity, by asking, "Do you intend to rule over us…?" They had to take the second dream seriously because repetition of a dream validates it,[18] and they did not want to further validate it with an expressed interpretation. After the first dream, "they hated him" [37:8] for arrogating royalty to himself. After the second, "they were jealous of him" [37:11] over the greatness and the rulership the validated dream foretold. When Yosef saw the brothers were silent, he told it to his father in their presence, intending for his father to interpret it. Yaakov's response, while scolding Yosef, was intended to establish the dream.

What were the "words" that caused them to hate him more? Rashi credits the "evil report" even though this happened earlier. This can be explained by the new event, the dream, triggering a new assessment of the earlier event, the evil report, resulting in even more hatred. Ramban credits the "words" Yosef employed to

---

17. 41:13: Just as he interpreted for us, thus it was.
18. 41:32: The repetition of the dream to Paro is because it is true, from God. See Ibn Ezra, ad loc., and Ber. 55b: In three ways dreams are established…. Some say repetition.

represent the dream, which glorified him over his brothers. The scene is set for the tragic events to unfold.

MDK: I find this selection easier to comprehend with the following schema:

Incitement	Response
Report to father	*None*
Tunic of fine wool	*They hated him*
First dream – sheaves:	
First mention	*They hated him more*
Elaboration	*They hated him more, for his dreams and for his words*
Second dream – sun, etc.	*They were jealous*

SELF-INDULGENCE INFLAMES
THE EVIL INCLINATION

> 37:12. And the brothers went to pasture their
> father's flock in Shechem.

Rashi: The word et *has dots above the letters, indicating they went only to "pasture" [indulge] themselves* [BR 84:13].

Gur Arye: Grammatically, *et* indicates the object of a transitive verb. The dots of the Masoretic text uproot the word,[19] eliminating the object "flock." Why not just delete the dotted word? The answer is, the brothers surely told their father that the purpose of their journey was to pasture the flock. An alternative answer is that leaving out *et* does not delete the object, "flocks," as *et* can be omitted, and with the object in place it could not be interpreted "pasture themselves."

What moral lesson can we learn from this midrash? What is the point of telling it to us? It was to inform us that the brothers set out not to sin, but to have a good time eating and drinking. When a person indulges himself, the evil inclination provokes

---

19. See Rashi 18:9. Mizrachi, ad loc.: Raban Shimon ben Gamliel said, whenever there are more letters than dots, delete the dotted letters and interpret the remaining word, unless there are more dotted than undotted letters, in which case the word formed by the dotted letters is interpreted. In our case, the entire word is dotted, meaning it, as well as the object it indicates, does not exist.

him, and in the end he will come to sin.[20] That is the moral lesson of the dots on *et*.

MDK: Maharal turns a grammar lesson into a morality play.

---

20. Rashi, Deut. 11:17: Beware – when you eat and become satiated, do not kick [at Hashem], for man does not rebel against Hashem unless he is satiated. Or Chadash, 143a, on the midrash, Est. R. 7:25: Hashem said to the tribes [Yosef's brothers]: "You sold your brother while eating and drinking – Haman will seize you while eating and drinking." On account of self-indulgent eating and drinking, the head becomes light, and that is how the brothers came to do this aberrant, unnatural act. Netiv Derech Eretz 1, 2:250a: Excessive eating confuses the *sechel* [intelligence, spirituality], as is well known. See also Or Chadash 90b, Chidushei Agadot on B.B. 12b, 3:67b, and Netiv Koach Hayetzer 1, 2:122b.

GAVRIEL'S MISSION

37:16. And a man found him, and, behold, he [Yosef] was lost in the field, and the man asked him, "What are you seeking?"

Rashi: The "man" is the angel Gavriel.

Gur Arye: What difference does it make in the story that Yosef was first lost? And why does the verse tell us that the "man" found him? The verse is telling us that Hashem is involved through His messenger, Gavriel. Had the angel not directed him to his brothers, Yosef would have returned home. We know this angel is Gavriel, for he is called "the man" [Dan. 9:21]. Gavriel means the power of God, from *gevura* [strength]. He is the one sent to destroy Sedom [B.M. 86a], and to save Chananya, Mishael, and Azaria from the fiery furnace [Dan. 9:21].[21] Yosef did not ask if the "man" knew where his brothers were. Instead he said, "Tell me where they are," for he knew that the angel knew.[22] This all comes to tell us of Hashem's hand in the story.

MDK: The narrative, without the embellishment by the rabbis, has entranced civilization for millenia. Chazal focus in on every textual nuance to add color and texture to the story.

---

21. Ex. 15:3: Hashem is a Man [*ish*] of War. Gur Arye, Deut. 1:13: The term *ish* is used in the context of strength and fear of sin. Also Gur Arye, Ex. 17:10: *Ish* applies to strength, as it is written [Kings I 2:2], "You shall become strengthened and be a man [*ish*]."
22. See Ramban 19:12.

LEGAL PRETEXTS

37:17. And the man said, "They traveled from here, for I heard them say, 'Let us go to Dotan.'"

Rashi: They moved themselves from a state of brotherhood. Dotan connotes conspiracies of laws [datot], legal pretexts to kill their brother.

Gur Arye: This midrash is based on an apparent redundancy. If he heard them say where they were going, why does Gavriel tell Yosef that they "traveled from here?" The answer is that he was warning him of the brothers' plot to kill him, and that their movement was away from brotherhood. Why then did Gavriel tell Yosef he heard them say, "let us go to Dotan?" The answer is that he was telling what he heard – that they were seeking legal pretexts [*datot*] to kill their brother.

MDK: Gavriel, Hashem's hand in the story, informs Yosef where to go to meet his brothers, while warning him to beware of his brothers' intentions. We are not told why Yosef did not heed the warning.

FLICKERINGS

> 37:33. And he [Yaakov] recognized it and he said,
> "It is my son's cloak. A wild animal has eaten him.
> Yosef has certainly been torn to bits."

Rashi: The Holy Spirit flickered within him. Without knowing it, Yaakov was prophesying Yosef's fate, that he would be provoked by Potifar's wife. Why did Hashem not reveal that Yosef was alive? The brothers had placed a ban, and cursed anyone who revealed this secret, and included Hashem in the ban.

Gur Arye: We learn from the seeming repetition of the idea that he was torn to death another point – that the wild animal referred to was a spark of prophecy of Yosef's test with Potifar's wife. This does not conflict with Rashi [45:27], that later when "Yaakov's spirit came alive," the Divine Presence was restored to him, for such "flickerings" of the Holy Spirit do not require the Divine Presence. Yaakov lost the Divine Presence on account of mourning and depression, as "the Divine Presence does not reside in the midst of depression, but rather amidst the joy of the fulfillment of the commandments" [Shab. 30b].[23] The flickerings served no purpose since Yaakov did not understand them, but because Yaakov was perpetually prepared for the Holy Spirit, it was never far from him. If so, why does He withhold knowledge of Yosef's survival? Here Rashi brings the midrash of the ban that even Hashem honored.

Why did Hashem honor the ban? Surely, the saintly Yaakov asked Him what happened to his son! Is it not so that "the will of those who fear Him, He will do, and their cries He will heed,

---

23. Netiv Hatorah 18, 1:75b: As Hashem is *shalem*, He connects only with people who are *shalem*, such as those who rejoice in the performance of His commandments. See Rambam, Eight Chapters, Ch. 7.

and He will save them" [Ps. 145:19]?[24] It is clear why the brothers wanted the ban – to avoid retribution by their father. If Hashem would agree even momentarily, the ban would go into effect,[25] as without Reuven and Binyamin, nine brothers required a tenth, Hashem, to convert the ban to an immutable oath that Yaakov's prayer could not reverse [Tanchuma, Vayeshev 2].[26] The nine brothers knew Hashem was there with them, because He is the *Makom* [Omnipresent, the place or space of the Universe].[27] In the words of the midrash [Pirke Derabbi Eliezer 38], "they made the *Makom* a partner with them." Hashem agreed with the brothers that if he would discover how Yosef came to be sold into slavery, Yaakov's powerful curse might destroy the brothers, who were the pillars of the Universe, and in so doing, destroy the world.[28]

Rav Yosef Colon agrees Hashem wanted to validate the ban on anyone telling Yaakov of Yosef's fate, but for a different reason [Maharik 37]. Yaakov needed punishment for failing to honor his parents for 22 years, as Rashi notes [37:34].

A third and most fitting reason for Hashem to honor the ban is "what a righteous person decrees, Hashem fulfills" [Ta'an. 23a].

---

24. See 30:3[6], Yerushalmi, Ta'an. 3:10, Shab. 63a, Netiv Hatorah 16, 1:71b, and Derech Hachaim 1:4, 75a.

25. Gur Arye, Num. 20:12: There are three stages, before the decree, after the decree, before the oath, and after the oath, at which time prayer and crying have no effect. Chidushei Agadot on R.H. 18a, 1:118b: The oath is the establishment of the decree. The sages said [Shebu. 36a] immediately reiterating a decree makes it an immutable oath, impossible to rend asunder.

26. Ber. 47b: Nine and *aron* [ark] combine to make a *minyan* [quorum of ten]. Gra: *Aron* is an abbreviated *echad roe v'eino nir'e* [One who sees but is not seen, i.e., Hashem]. See Rashi 18:28 and Gevurot Hashem 13:68b.

27. BR 68:9: Why is Hashem's name expressed as *Makom*? He is the place of the Universe! It is not just that the Universe is His. See 1:1[19]{77}.

28. Pesikta Rabati 3: Yosef, in addition to failing to inform his father of his own fate for 22 years, avoided his father after the latter came down to Egypt. He was careful not to be alone with his father, fearing having to answer the awesome question,"What did your brothers do to you?" If Yaakov knew the truth, he would curse them and destroy the world.

Although the psalmist said [Ps. 147:19], "He tells His words to Yaakov," these words He did not tell him. The ban of the brothers, validated by the partnership, was accepted by Hashem Himself, and realizing this, Reuven, Binyamin, Yitzchak, and Yosef all kept the brother's secret.

MDK: The first reason given for the ban on informing Yaakov of the sale of Yosef by his brothers, that Yaakov would curse his sons on hearing the story, is most cogent. The brothers were in mortal fear of retribution, and Hashem agreed, knowing that if such a curse on his sons would occur, Hashem would have to honor it. Given their role in the future of the world, this would be tantamount to a reversal of creation. The stakes could not have been higher.

THE CONSOLATION THAT FAILED

37:35. And all his sons and daughters came up to console him, but he refused to be consoled...

Rashi: A person cannot accept consolation for a person he thinks is dead but is actually alive. It is only upon the dead that it has been decreed that they will be forgotten, not upon the living.

Gur Arye: If Yaakov was unable to accept consolation, why didn't he draw the conclusion his son was alive? One answer is that the decree to forget the dead has no set time,[29] and a person may be affected by an emotional state. Yaakov blamed himself and his mental state for his inability to be consoled.

Let us examine this proposition. A completely righteous person should not have such a character flaw that he could not accept consolation.[30] It is forbidden to torment oneself. The *Gemara* [Ned. 10a] tells us a *nazir* is called a sinner for denying himself wine, how much more so a person who torments himself. This cannot be the correct answer. Rather, perhaps because there was no body, Yaakov did not cease to search for it, never giving up on eventual burial. As long as the search continued, the uncertainty continued, as one does not begin to count the seven days of mourning in the absence of a body until the mourner despairs of the prospect of burial.[31] However if this were the case, it should say, "he did not mourn." Instead, the text says, "he refused to be consoled."

The real reason he refused consolation was that his son was

---

29. Pes. 54b: Seven things are hidden from a person: the day of his death, the day of his consolation...
30. M.K. 27b: Rav Huna sent a woman who was mourning excessively a message to cease her mourning.
31. Rambam, Laws of Mourning 1:2.

not dead! Consolation comes with closure, and there was no closure.

MDK: Gur Arye sees a problem with Rashi's explanation. Yaakov knew the "rules" of how a dead person is forgotten. He could have deduced Yosef was alive! The answer given is he did not trust himself, attributing his failure to be consoled to an emotional aberration. Gur Arye refutes this answer, restates Rashi's proposition, and leaves his incisive question unanswered. Perhaps the next selection helps to answer it.

IMMUNITY FROM GEHINNOM

37:35. ...and he said, "For I will go *sheola* [to the grave, to Hell] mourning over my son..."

Rashi: Sheola in its simple sense means "to the grave," meaning I will be buried in my mourning, and will not be consoled all my life. According to the midrash, it means Gehinnom. A sign was given over to Yaakov from the Almighty: "if none of my sons die in my lifetime, I am assured I will not see Gehinnom" [Tanchuma, Vayigash 9].

Gur Arye: Man's judgment in Gehinnom is twelve months long [Shab. 32b], and if all twelve sons are alive when Yaakov dies, *Gehinnom* will have no power over him. The nation of Israel is considered one body with twelve parts. The twelve tribes correspond to the twelve astrological signs, the twelve months of the year, the twelve hours in the day, and the twelve stones Aharon wore.[32]

According to this midrash, Yosef's death makes him subject to *Gehinnom*, and he believed that Yosef had been killed. He could not be consoled, for now he thought he faced *Gehinnom*.[33]

MDK: A recurrent theme in Yaakov's narrative – that his sins may have rendered him unworthy – occurs again here. He assumes he deserves Gehinnom *for his unspecified sins, and having been stripped of his protection by Yosef's death, is now doomed.*

---

32. Netzach Yisrael 37:164a. See Tanchuma Yashan, Vayeshev 8.
33. Netiv Ha'avoda 9, 1:103a: When the *Gemara* states, "Anyone who reads *Shema* and takes care with every letter, *Gehinnom* is cooled off for him" [Ber. 15b], this is because he accepts upon himself His Kingship and His Oneness. It is known that *Gehinnom* was created on the second day [BR 4:8]. Accepting Hashem's Oneness by carefully reading the *Shema* cancels the power of *Gehinnom*. This explanation is true and proper for believers. Ibid., 7, 1:99a: The twelve tribes are like Yaakov, for through Yaakov they formed a complete unity, as the twelve plus their father make thirteen, which is the *gematria* of *echad*. Yaakov's "one" amidst his sons fends off *Gehinnom*.

YITZCHAK HONORS THE BAN

37:36. ...and his father cried for him.

Rashi: Yitzchak cried on account of Yaakov's distress, but did not mourn, for he knew Yosef was alive.

Gur Arye: Yitzchak honored the brothers' ban on telling the secret of Yosef's fate, saying to himself, "how can I reveal the secret if Hashem does not to reveal it" [Rashi 37:33]. "His father" must refer to Yitzchak, not Yaakov, for Yaakov was mourning already, and crying precedes mourning rather than vice versa. If Yitzchak did not know that Yosef was alive, he would have cried "with" his son, not "for" him.

Mizrachi asks how Yitzchak came to know the secret. The answer is, "prophets do not lose their counsel" [Jer. 18:18] – Hashem told him, and Binyamin as well.[34] Also, "Hashem's secrets are for those that fear Him" [Ps. 25:12], which is interpreted by the *Gemara* [Shab. 77b, Hag. 3b, Sanh. 48b, Nid. 20b] to mean that the sages know things hidden from other people. The ban only applied to telling Yaakov. Hashem did not want him to know for twenty-two years, corresponding to the twenty-two years he failed to honor his parents [Rashi 37:33].

MDK: Three reasons were cited above [Gur Arye, 36:33] for Hashem's signing on to the ban, and here Maharal brings the second reason, that of Colon [the Maharik], that Hashem kept the ban to punish Yaakov for not honoring his parents.

---

34. See Midrash Shocher Tov, Ps. 15:7.

AN ENCOUNTER AT THE CROSSROADS

38:15. And Yehuda saw her, and thought she was
a harlot.

Rashi: Because she sat at the crossroads.

Gur Arye: How could Yehuda consider patronizing harlotry permissible? The Torah says [Deut. 23:18], "There shall not be a harlot among the daughters of Israel."[35] One explanation is that he "married" her with the pledge he gave her. This is clearly in error, as the law is established [Kid. 8a] that pledged money does not accomplish *kidushin* [marriage, dedication to one man, sanctification]. Also, Yehuda was ready to go to her without payment, till she asked for it. Furthermore, she asked for the pledge as a proof of paternity, not to become married to him.

People are recognized in three ways – one, by their individualized appearance; two, by their clothing; and three, by their craft. The first is image, by which he is identified; the second is another aspect of image, as a man is described by clothing [see Isa. 63:1]. The third, craft, is not image, but is the way a person is known. Tamar asked him for his signet ring [38:18], his personal seal, which was like his identity, the way a signature testifies to a person's identity. She asked him for his cloak, by which he was recognized. And she asked for his staff, his regal scepter, the proof of his rulership, as it is written [49:10], "the scepter shall not pass from Yehuda."[36] Kingship was his craft.

---

35. Mizrachi: Although Rambam and Ra'avad disagree [Laws of Marriage 1:4], in the case of sexual relations outside of marriage, as to whether the couple transgresses the prohibition of *kedesha* [harlotry] and is liable to *malkut* [lashes], both agree that a woman dedicated to harlotry and available to all is a *kedesha* and subject to *malkut*.

36. Radak 49:10: He rules over his people and admonishes them with scepter in hand. See Est. 5:2 and Ramban 38:18.

Another way to look at the three pledges is to consider the three effects of children on their parents:

One, they prevent erasure of one's name from Israel.[37]

Two, they extend the person the way a branch extends a tree,[38] resulting in *shelemut* [harmony, completion].

Three, the child aids and supports the parent, and after 120 years, buries her, as the *Gemara* says, "a stick for her hand and a shovel for her grave" [Yeb. 65b].

The signet ring represents the continuation of his name. *P'tilcha* [your cloak, your fringes] represent the extensions of his person, for it is known that children are compared to fringes – just as fringes extend from a man's garment, children extend from his body, which is the garment of his soul.[39] The third item, the staff, is what the son is to the father who leans on him. The three pledges alluded to children, by which she showed him her intent was not immoral.

Perhaps she was hinting that he should marry her – one, that his name [signet ring] should not be erased;[40] two, that she could provide him with additional "fringes," children to replace his lost sons, and to fulfill the commandment to reproduce;[41] and three, that if they have children, he would have a "staff for his hand" in her later years.

The question remains, how was it permissible for him to have sexual relations with her if he thought her to be a harlot? He said, "Get yourself ready, let me come to you" [38:16], asking her consent

---

37. See Deut. 25:6; Rashi, Gen. 16:2; and 5:28[3].

38. See Gevurot Hashem 9:57b and Derasha Leshabbat Hagadol 201a.

39. See Netiv Ha'avoda, 15, 1:123a.

40. Deut. 25:6: that his name not be erased.

41. Yeb. 61b: Bet Hillel holds the fulfillment of "be fruitful and multiply" requires a son and a daughter, while Bet Shamai holds two sons suffice. This law applies only to the permissibility of not marrying after loss of one's wife.

and implying she not act in an immoral way. He was asking her to be singularly dedicated to him, as a concubine.[42] She agreed.

We know Tamar was a righteous woman, from her modesty[43] and from her willingness to die by fire rather than embarrass Yehuda [Rashi 38:25]. How could she, the daughter of a *kohen*,[44] make herself available to her father-in-law, the punishment for which is death by burning? It seems the daughter-in-law prohibition for the sons of Noach does not extend beyond the death of her husband.[45] She was, then, permissible to Yehuda and consented to be dedicated to him as his concubine. Thus there was no sin on her part.

On what grounds did Yehuda sentence his pregnant daughter-in-law to death by burning [38:24]? This is the penalty for a sexually immoral daughter of a *kohen*, but only applies if she is married or betrothed [Rashi, Lev. 21:9]. Ramban here discusses the nature of the marital attachment of a *shomeret yavam* [woman awaiting levirate marriage] and concludes the law does not apply to Noachides [Sanh. 58a], and especially here, as Yehuda instituted levirate marriage the first time [BR 85:5]. He sentenced her to burning for another reason, the same reason the sons of Yaakov killed Shechem, son of Chamor – sexual immorality, as they said [34:7], "They committed a travesty against Israel, to have sexual relations with a daughter of Israel, and such a thing is not done." After the flood, the nations of the world fenced themselves from immorality by imposing the death penalty for sexual infractions

---

42. Ra'avad, Laws of Marriage, 1:4: If she singularly dedicates herself to one man, there are no lashes and no prohibition – she is the concubine mentioned in the Torah [25:6]. Rambam disagrees.
43. Meg. 10b: Yehuda did not recognize her, because she covered her face when she was in her father-in-law's house.
44. Rashi 38:24: She was the daughter of Shem, who was a *kohen*.
45. Rambam, Laws of Forbidden Relations, 14:10: A gentile man is forbidden to have sexual relations with his mother, the wife of his father, his sister born of his mother, married women, males, and animals.

[Rashi 34:7].[46] In this case, burning was chosen as an appropriate punishment for the daughter of a priest. This was the law promulgated by the court of Shem the son of Noach, who happened to be her father and a priest [14:18]. Ramban concludes her sin was to shame the ruler of the land, but this is erroneous, as the *Gemara* clearly states [A.Z. 36b], "The death penalty for illicit sexual relations was decreed by the court of Shem, as it is written, 'Take her out and burn her.'"

We must establish whether Tamar was a *penuya* [free of any marital attachment] and available to offer herself to Yehuda, or not. Rav Shmuel bar Nachmani says [Sot. 10a], "She sat at the crossroads" means she exonerated herself from sin, an orphan, whose relative other than her father married her off while she was a child. As she refused the unconsummated marriage when she reached adulthood, she was free to couple with Yehuda. This interpretation does not square with the *Gemara* [Yeb. 34b], that is, that the sin of both Er and Onan was to have coitus interruptus with her in order that she not lose her beauty through childbearing – if she was mature she did not refuse the marriage, and if she was immature she could not conceive! To answer this, consider that her marriage to Er was subject to her later refusal when she reached adulthood, but when he died she was also subject to levirate marriage to Onan. When Onan died, she exerted her right of refusal of the original marriage to Er, and declared herself free and clear of any marital attachment, and available to Yehuda.

Alternatively, before the giving of the Torah, a Noachide father-in-law could fulfill levirate marriage with his daughter-in-law, and the prohibition of relations with a daughter-in-law is pushed aside in the same way as the Torah tells us to push aside the sister-in-law prohibition [Lev. 18:16] in the case of the usual levirate marriage. Accordingly, Tamar consummated her levirate marital attachment to Yehuda in a fully permissible manner.

---

46. Mizrachi: We see her death penalty as a decree, rather than a Torah law.

MDK: This beautiful discourse deals with the halachic ramifications of the apparently problematic episode of Yehuda and Tamar. One by one, apparent violations of Torah law are confronted and meticulously explained to provide a rational framework for the behavior of these two righteous real people, who founded the family out of which would rise the royal House of David.

PREMONITIONS OF KINGS AND REDEEMERS

> 38:25. ...I have conceived by the man to whom
> these items belong...Please recognize whose
> things these are.

Rashi: Please [na] *implies pleading. I beg of you, recognize your Creator, and do not destroy three lives.*

Gur Arye: "Three lives" implies the mother and two babies. How did she know she was carrying twins? Possibly she knew that the kingship of the Jewish people would arise out of Yehuda,[47] and kingship is compared to the moon, and the moon is paired with the sun. The moon needs a sun to produce the light that the moon reflects.[48] Ramban [38:29] cites the midrash of Nechunia ben Hakana [Sefer Habahir 196] explaining the meaning of the names Tamar gave her twin sons. Zerach [*shining*] refers to the sun, which always shines, never ceasing the production of its radiant energy. Peretz [breaking forth] refers to the moon, which waxes and wanes, at times full, and at times completely undone. The dominion of the House of David is comparable to the dominion of the moon. The moon is called small [1:16] and David is called small [Sam. 1 17:14]. The twenty-eight days of the moon's light correspond to the twenty-eight generations from Peretz to Tzidkiahu. The fifteen days of the moon's ascendancy correspond to the fifteen generations from Avraham to David, and the fifteen days of the moon's decline correspond to the fifteen generations from Rechavam to Yechonia. The variability of the power of the

---

47. Rashi, Sot. 10a: Hashem issued an everlasting decree that kings would emanate from this woman, Tamar. And it is impossible for the kings to emanate from anyone but Yehuda, as it is written, "Yehuda is a young lion" [49:9].

48. Derech Hachaim 1:1, 19b: Yehoshua is the singular recipient with respect to Moshe, as the rabbis said [B.B. 75a], "Moshe's face is like the face of the sun, and Yehoshua's face is like the face of the moon," and it is known that the moon receives its radiance from the sun.

moon corresponds to the variability of the power of the House of David. Even when the moon loses its light, it always returns renewed, just like the House of David will return renewed and lead us out of our present exile, speedily in our days.[49]

According to the midrash [BR 85:10], Tamar knew she was carrying kings and redeemers, for she would place a kerchief on her belly and say, "I'm pregnant with kings, I'm pregnant with redeemers." If she knew this, we shouldn't be surprised she knew she was carrying twins.

MDK: Maharal leaves implicit and undiscussed the major moral lesson to focus on a single troublesome word in the midrash – three. Tamar is ready to face death by burning rather than embarrass Yehuda by accusing him in public. Yehudah rises to the task and admits the tokens she quietly presents are his. The actions of both of them establish their credentials as progenitors of the royal House of David and King Messiah. All this is not commented upon, but rather Tamar's mention of three lives in the midrash provokes an analysis of Tamar as prophetess and the character of this important person, who gets only a few lines mention in the Torah text.

---

49. Chidushei Agadot on R.H. 25a, 1:127b.

DAVID, KING OF ISRAEL, LIVES AND ENDURES

> 38:28–30. And it was when she gave birth, and
> he put out a hand, and the midwife took and
> tied a red thread on his hand, saying "this came
> out first." And it was as he retracted his hand,
> and, behold, his brother emerged, and she said,
> "With what strength you asserted yourself!" and
> she called his name Peretz. And afterward, his
> brother emerged, on whose hand was the red
> thread, and she called his name Zerach.

Rashi: The word hand [yad] *is written four times, corresponding to the four bans violated by Achan, who descended from him* [Jos. 7:21]. *Some say the four hands correspond to the four things Achan took – a Babylonian cloak, two pieces of silver weighing 200 shekels, and an old ingot* [BR 85:14].

Gur Arye: Why refer to Achan here? Something important is happening here, hidden and mystical. These weren't ordinary sons, but, rather, were born at Hashem's decree.[50] From Peretz was fitting to emerge the kingship of the House of David, and from Zerach, Achan, who violated the bans. The description of the unusual birth teaches this to us. Who ever heard of a baby extending and retracting his hand? Zerach tried to enter the world reaching and grabbing, but Peretz was even more aggressive, pushing himself ahead to attain firstborn status.[51] The kingship will go to the one who broke forth, Peretz, for a king seizes what he wants or needs legally, by right of eminent domain, as the *Mishna* says [Sanh. 20b] that the king may break down fences to make a road.

---

50. See 38:5[3]<36>.
51. Rashi 25:26: A necessary and sufficient condition for the end of Esav's reign is that Yaakov be standing ready to take it over. We see this from Yaakov grasping Esav's heel.

The *Gemara* there goes on to explain that he is permitted to take anything mentioned in the section on the king [Sam. I 8:11–18], up to and including your sons and daughters. The second one, Zerach, through his descendant Achan, will also use the power of his hand to take, but he will be stealing something forbidden. Peretz and Zerach are the moon and the sun, both rulers,[52] both kings,[53] each legally possessing the right of eminent domain, but not to the excessive application of that right by seizing something forbidden to him. Zerach, the shining sun, disqualifies himself by overreaching, as the four hands referring to Achan symbolize.

Peretz, the moon, was fitting to be progenitor of the kingship of the House of David.[54] It may wax and wane,[55] as some of the kings were true to Hashem and some were not, and it may seem to disappear for a period of time, as we are experiencing in our current exile on account of our many sins.

MDK: When the Romans prohibited transmission of notification of the new moon, the rabbis [R.H. 25a] used the expression, "David, King of Israel, lives and continues to exist" to let the world know the new moon was declared. And when we see and sanctify the new moon in its ascendancy each month, we take comfort in declaring three times that just as the moon has reappeared, David will reappear in the form of his descendant, Mashiach. May he come speedily in our day. David, King of Israel, lives and continues to exist!

---

52. 1:16:…the large luminary to rule the day, and the small luminary to rule the night. Siddur, Shabbat Shacharit: Power and strength He put in them to be rulers in the midst of the earth.

53. Rashi 1:19: The moon complained, "Is it possible for two kings to use one crown?"

54. Ruth 4:18–22: And these are the generations of Peretz: Peretz begot Chetzron. And Chetzron begot Ram, and Ram begot Aminadav, and Aminadav begot Nachshon, and Nachshon begot Salma. And Salma begot Boaz, and Boaz begot Oved. And Oved begot Yishai, and Yishai begot David.

55. See Ramban, postscript to *Vezot Haberacha* and Rabbenu Bechaye 38:29.

Miketz

> 42:2. And he said, "Behold, I heard that there is
> food in Egypt. Go down there and provide for us
> from there, and we will live and not die.

Rashi: The verse says *redu* [go down] rather than *lechu* [go], hinting at the 210 years that they served Egypt, corresponding to the
gematria [numerical equivalence] of *redu*.

Gur Arye: It would be more appropriate for the verb to be the
more positive "go" than the negative "go down," a language that
means descent. Yaakov, signaling the inception of a new stage
of the history of his people, might have chosen a more positive
verb. Hashem's first utterance in the Torah is "Let there be light!"
and David tells us, "The introduction of your words illuminate"
[Ps. 119:130], interpreted by the rabbis [Ex. R. 50:1] to mean that
the righteous begin their speech with light. Yaakov's term *redu*
must be telling us something that supersedes the principle of the
illuminating, positive introduction. Rashi's midrash supplies the
message – 210 years.

The Land of Israel is the highest of all the lands,[1] and the Holy
Temple is the highest point in the Land of Israel. How can this
be? Surely Mt. Hermon is taller than Mt. Moriah, and Switzerland

---

1.   Deut. 17:8: And you will arise and ascend to the Place Hashem will choose.

has more altitude than the Land of Israel! This can be understood in terms of spirituality. Consider that the Earth is a sphere, say, a rubber ball floating on top of the water. If there is a spot on the surface of the ball that is lighter than the rest of the ball, that spot will rise to the top. Spirituality has no linear dimension and no mass, and the place in it is concentrated is lighter and rises to the top. Therefore, no matter where you come from on the face of the Earth, you are making *aliya* [rising] when you come to the Land of Israel. This is what is meant in the *Mishna* [Kid. 69a], "Ten genealogical classes rose [*alu*] from Bavel,"[2] on which Rashi comments "the Land of Israel is higher than all the other lands."[3]

MDK: First, Gur Arye tells us what is troubling Rashi, that "go" would be preferable to "go down" because Yaakov would want to start this new chapter on a positive note. Rashi answers that the numerical message – 210 – makes redu *the preferred verb. Elsewhere, in the* Gemara *[Kid. 69a], the opposite of* redu *–* alu *– is employed to convey going up to the Land of Israel. Maharal there gives another reason why* redu *is the proper verb – the Land of Israel, on account of its spirituality, is higher than any other land.*

---

2. Chidushei Agadot on Kid. 69a, 2:157b.
3. Chidushei Agadot on Kid. 69a, 2:147b.

THE COMMANDMENT TO TEACH YOUR
CHILDREN THE HOLY TONGUE

42:23. And they did not know that Yosef heard,
for the interpreter was between them.

Rashi: The interpreter was Menashe.

Gur Arye: We know this from the *heh hayedia* [definite article] in
hamelitz [the interpreter]. Menashe could interpret for them, for
he knew Egyptian and Hebrew. His father was obligated to teach
him the Holy Tongue, as it is written, "And you shall teach your
son to speak of them…" [Deut. 11:19], which Sifri interprets, "From
the time the toddler starts to speak,[4] the father speaks with him
in the Holy Tongue and teaches him Torah."[5] The interceder must

---

4. Suk. 42a: The father's obligation to teach his son the Holy Tongue begins
   when the son knows how to speak, which is age three. See Rashi, Ab. 5:21 and
   Tanchuma, Kedoshim 14.

5. Sifri continues: "If he fails to speak to him in the Holy Tongue and to teach
   him Torah, he is considered to have buried him, as it says, 'and you shall
   teach them to your children and speak of them…in order that their days will
   increase,' implying that if you do not they will die." Tosefta Hag. 1:2: "When a
   child knows enough to speak, his father teaches him *Shema*, Torah, and the
   Holy Tongue. Otherwise, it would be better for the child not have come into
   the world." However, the requirement to teach Hebrew is omitted in Suk. 42a:
   When he knows enough to speak, his father teaches him Torah and the reading of the *Shema*. The textual discrepancy as to whether teaching your child
   Hebrew is a positive Torah commandment is answered in two ways by the
   Torah Temima, Deut 11:19 [52]: The *mitzvah* of teaching one's son the Holy
   Tongue may apply only in the Land of Israel when the Jewish People are resid-
   ing on their own land, whereas in our present exile it is impossible for most
   people to keep it. However, it does not sit well that the entire matter be up-
   rooted from the law. Perhaps the rabbis took heed of Rabbi Eliezer's deathbed
   admonition to his students, after suffering many years of excommunication
   [Pes. 28a]: "Restrain your children from *higayon* [reason, logic] and seat them
   between the knees of wise teachers of Torah," which Rashi explains, "do not
   translate texts more than necessary." This may limit their access to texts that

be someone we already know, as signified by the definite article, and who can speak both the Egyptian and the Hebrew tongue. It cannot be Efraim, who was born in the year before the famine [Radak 41:7] and was not yet three,[6] the age at which Yosef would have taught him the Holy Tongue. It must be Menashe.

they may interpret for themselves, resulting in their knowledge being something other than the received wisdom of our sages. For this reason the biblical injunction to teach children the Holy Tongue may have been deemphasized.

6. 45:7: This is the second year of the famine...

Vayigash

DESTRUCTION AS SEEN FROM THE PAST AND THE FUTURE

45:14. And he fell upon tzavarei [*the neck of, or technically, necks of*] *his brother Binyamin, and he cried, and Binyamin cried on* tzavarav [*his neck, or technically, necks*].

Rashi: Yosef cried on account of the future destruction of the two Holy Temples that would be in Binyamin's territory. Binyamin cried for the destruction of the Sanctuary at Shilo that would be in Yosef's territory.

Gur Arye: Rashi's midrash [BR 93:12] answers the question, "How many necks did Binyamin have?" The plurality of necks is a reference to the two reasons he cried. The problem with this midrash is that Yosef apparently also had two necks, but only one reason for Binyamin to cry. Radak explains in his Book of Roots [*tzadi, vav, resh*] that the neck is referred to in the plural because there are two sides to the neck. This, of course, calls into question the initial reasoning of the midrash, which requires that Yosef have one neck.

Rav Eliahu Mizrachi of Constantinople has an answer that fits the midrash. In his Torah text, the *tzavarav* of Yosef at the end of the verse lacks a *yud*, clearly referring to a singular neck! The problem with this explanation is that all our Torah texts have a *yud* in *tzavarav*.

I think the neck positioned at the junction of the unpaired head structures [head, nose, mouth] and the paired body structures [arms, legs, ribs] can be singular, as in [41:42], "he put a gold chain on her neck," or plural as in our verse. Although both "necks" in our verse are pluralized through the use of a *yud*, the *yud* of Binyamin's neck is pronounced [*tzavarei*], while the *yud* of Yosef's [*tzavarav*] is not. Thus the midrash knows that Binyamin's portion would have two reasons to cry, and Yosef's portion would have one.

Consider that this verse relates to the once and future reunion of long lost brothers, marked by weeping over the loss of the Holy Temples and Shilo. After Yeravam ben Nevat split off the ten northern tribes to form the Kingdom of Israel [Kings I 11:31], Binyamin was one of the tribes remaining in the Kingdom of Judea, and can be seen to represent Yehuda. Yeravam arose from the tribe of Efraim, the son of Yosef [Kings I 11:26], and his kingdom was eventually exiled by Sancheriv [Kings II 17: 6–18]. Hashem promises redemption and reunion of the ten tribes with the remainder of the Jewish People [Ezek. 37:17]. He also promises, "They will come with weeping and with pleading I will transport them" [Jer. 31:8], and the midrash states [BR 93:12], "Just as Yosef appeased his brothers only with weeping, thus the Holy One, blessed be He, will redeem Israel in the midst of weeping." The reunion of Yosef and Binyamin foretells the reunion of Yosef with Yehuda and Israel with Judea in the end of days. May it come swiftly in our time.

MDK: A dispassionate analysis would conclude that the answer of the Mizrachi is clearly more logical than that of Maharal. Perhaps the author of the midrash had the Constantinople text. Maharal must have had his reasons for not considering a Torah text other than the one he had to possibly be correct. That would open a new can of worms. We should not be surprised at rare versions of the

Masoretic text. For example, Rashi had an inverted nun *at the end of* Parashat Noach. *This idea shakes one's confidence in the "Bible Codes."*

But let us focus on the novel poetic notion that the crying at the reunion of the brothers foretells the crying at the reunion of their descendants in the time of the Mashiach.

THE DEEPER MESSAGE OF THE WAGONS

> 45:27. And he saw the wagons which Yosef sent to transport him, and the spirit of Yaakov their father came alive.

Rashi: Yosef sent a message to his father encoded in the agalot *[wagons, but can also mean female calves]. Just before their long separation, they had been studying the law of egla arufa [the broken neck calf], which Yaakov was reminded of by the wagons [agalot].*

Gur Arye: There was a reason why Yaakov and Yosef were discussing this particular law. Da'at Zekenim Miba'alei Hatosafot note that Yosef was sent to Shechem from "Chevron Valley" [37:14], as Yaakov accompanied him from their home in Chevron to the valley below. Yosef told his father to return and not bother himself, but Yaakov insisted that *levaya* [accompaniment] is a very important mitzva that averts bloodshed. When a corpse is found between towns [Deut. 21:7], measurements are made to determine the nearest town, and elders of that town must perform the ceremony of the *egla arufa* in which they proclaim, "our hands did not spill this blood." The *Gemara* explains [Sot. 46b] that it is not that the elders were suspected of murder, rather that their proclamation avers that the victim did not leave their town unaccompanied, which teaches us that failure to accompany a person out of town is tantamount to murder. As a corollary to this, Rav Yehuda says in the name of Rav that if one accompanies his friend four *amot* in the city, his friend will be protected from harm. As Yosef was departing from Chevron Valley, Yaakov was teaching him this precept, secure that his accompaniment had guaranteed his son's safety. Then Yosef dissapears and Yaakov is despondent for twenty-two years. Yosef signals his father with the wagons [*agalot*] that the lesson of the *egla arufa* was true after all, that his father's accompaniment had saved him from harm's way. Yaakov's teaching was confirmed, and his spirit came alive.

MDK: *Rashi taught us that* Emek Chevron *meant "the profound advice of the saint buried in Chevron," referring to Avraham. In so doing, he distracted us from the simple meaning of the verse that Yaakov dispatched Yosef from the valley at the base of the mountain town where they lived. I was blinded by Rashi's midrash till his grandsons, the Ba'alei Tosafot, explained* emek *to me.*

THE SECRET OF SACRIFICE, THE SOD OF KORBAN

> 46:1. And Yisrael and all he had travelled and came to Beersheva, and he offered sacrifices to the God of his father Yitzchak.

Rashi: A person is obligated to honor his father more than his grandfather, so he designated the sacrifices to the God of Yitzchak and did not mention Avraham.

Gur Arye: Ramban asks why he didn't just say "the God of his forefathers," or, as he said before [32:10], "Hashem, the God of my father Avraham and the God of my father Yitzchak." The rabbis [BR 93:5] are not troubled by this question, as our verse deals with *korban* [sacrifice, coming close], through which one comes close and attaches oneself to Hashem.[1] This pertains particularly to Yitzchak on account of his role in the *akeda* [binding]. With respect to prayer, the merit of Avraham precedes that of Yitzchak [Ex. 32:13 and Deut. 9:27].[2]

In Avot [2:2], it is noted that Yitzchak merited the "column of *avoda* [service]," the second pillar on which the world stands, by virtue of having sacrificed himself on the altar, thereby bringing himself close to Hashem.[3] Yitzchak embodied *yir'a* [fear, awe], which derives from the relationship of the *Ila* [Prime Cause, Hashem] to the *alul* [resultant, creature, man] – man [*alul*] is insignificant in that he is totally dependent on the *Ila*. This fear is quite distinct from the love of Hashem, through which one comes to possess a complete connection with Him. However, *yir'a* brings

---

1. See Gur Arye, Ex. 21:1[3], Gevurot Hashem 8, 46a, and Netiv Ha'avoda 1, 1:77a.
2. Gur Arye, Lev. 26:42, where the order of the patriarchs is inverted: Hashem Himself mentions them in whatever order He chooses, but Moshe must keep to the proper order [Ex. 21:1] so as to collect the merits of all of them together.
3. Derech Hachaim 29a.

no connection, only self-abnegation.[4] *Korban* is the return of the *alul* to the *Ila*. Everything is nothing without Him, and sacrifice teaches us that. The books of the Pentateuch relate to the descriptions of Hashem: Genesis – *Gadol* [Great], Exodus – *Gibor* [Strong], Leviticus – *Nora* [Awesome].[5] The latter deals with sacrifice, the negation of something that is a proxy for the negation of self. Who better to embody this *yir'a* than Yitzchak!

MDK: A recurrent theme in Maharal is the juxtaposition of love and awe. Love is to awe as prayer is to sacrifice as Avraham is to Yitzchak. Both are needed.

---

4. Netiv Yirat Hashem 1, 2:21a.
5. Gevurot Hashem 68:216a.

SEX DETERMINATION

46:15. These are the sons of Lea which she bore
Yaakov in Padan Aram, and Dina, his daughter.

Rashi: The narrative makes the males depend on Lea and the female on Yaakov, to teach you that if a woman sows first she will bear a son, but if a man sows first she will bear a daughter [Nid. 31a].

Gur Arye: This verse delves into nothing less than the secret of sex determination. Mizrachi asks why Rashi brings the discussion here if it is explicitly stated [Lev. 12:2], "if a woman sows, she shall bear a male"? The answer is that our verse alludes to the converse corollary. One might think a woman's sowing first produces a male, but a man's sowing first could result in a male or a female. Our verse shows that the female results from the man sowing first.

How does this come to be? One erroneous answer relates the matter to Rav's opinion [Pes. 76a], "The upper one conquers the lower one." She sows first and her "seed" [ovum] finds its place. Then he sows, and his seed [sperm] finds and conquers the ovum, imprinting his maleness on the zygote.

This, however, is not the way of the world that Hashem, in His infinite wisdom, saw fit to create. The male is attracted to the female and combines with her to achieve *shelemut* just as she combines with him to achieve *shelemut*. Her sowing first imparts her effort and her affinity to the ovum, and her attraction to the male extends not just to her mate, but to her offspring as well. If he sows first, the converse applies. Each participant in the creative act strives for *hashlama* [harmonious completion], and the *hashlama* of each sex is the opposite sex.

There is an additional deep and remarkable point to be made here. The rabbis said [Nid. 31a], "There are three partners in the formation of the embryo: the father, the mother, and the Holy One, blessed be He." Hashem takes part in the formation of the sex of the child. He connects the male and female, placing His name in both of them, the *yud* in *ish* [man] and the *heh* in *isha* [woman] [Rashi, Sot. 17a]. If He would form the male from the male and the female from the female, this would not impart unity. He unites them by making the mother pass on the maleness and the father the femaleness. When the Torah states, "they will be one flesh" [2:24], it refers to the unity embodied in the embryo.

MDK: Rav's view of sexual union entails conquest of the female by the male. Maharal's view of sexual union is mutual fulfillment and attainment of shelemut, *a spiritual state of harmonious perfection.*

THE SAINTLY ONE RESPONDS IN HIS WAY

> 46:29. ...and he [Yaakov] appeared to him [Yosef], and he [Yosef] fell upon his neck, and continued to cry upon his neck.

Rashi: But Yaakov did not cry on Yosef's neck and did not kiss him. The rabbis comment that he was reading the shema *prayer, Hear, O Israel, the Lord is our God, the Lord is one [Deut. 5:1].*

Gur Arye: If Yaakov had to defer his reaction to the emotional re-union with his son after twenty-two years, there must have been some time-bound compelling reason. The reading of the *shema* might qualify, as the saintly ones perform each commandment at the earliest possible moment [Pes. 4a]. This should have applied to Yosef just as it did to Yaakov. The answer is Yosef said it as well, but he was required to interrupt when he saw his father. The law goes according to Rabbi Yehuda [Ber. 13a], that one must interrupt, even in the middle of a paragraph, to greet another for whom one has *yir'a* [awe], like a parent.

It is hard to imagine Yaakov containing his emotional response for such a seeming technicality. The *shema* in this context is not the twice-daily recitation, but rather an intense overwhelming emotional response. As he sees his long-lost son, now a viceroy, his heart fills with love and awe of the Holy One, blessed be He, how His qualities are Good and *Shalem*, and how He rewards those who fear Him.[6] This is the quality of the saintly – when something good happens to them, they attach to Hashem for the

---

6. Netiv Ahavat Hashem 1, 2:41a: Sifri on Deut. 6:4 says "and you shall love Hashem, your God, with all your heart" refers to Avraham, "and all your soul" refers to Yitzchak, "and all *meodecha* [your might, sounds like your thanks]" refers to the thanks of Yaakov, who said [32:11], "I am too small in the face of all the kindness." Avraham loved Hashem in that all his deeds were for the love of Hashem. However Yitzchak's attachment to Hashem was of a different nature – he negated his soul completely, tying himself on the altar. Yaakov's

Good and the Truth He did for them out of love[7] and awe.[8] This is the *shema,* in which is mentioned the Unity of the Kingdom of Heaven as well as the love of Him. It was quite fitting for Yaakov to recite the *shema* when Yosef came to him, considering the great pain endured on his account. Now, seeing him a viceroy generated a love for Hashem, who brought about this joyful moment after the most difficult straits, and Yaakov accepted His Kingship, the love of Him, and the awe of Him. This is the proper understanding of the story.

MDK: Everyone's sins, for "there is no righteous man on earth who will do only good and not sin." Hashem's Attribute of Strict Judgment neccessitates for punishment and bad things to happen, and the same Hashem's Attribute of Mercy necessitates forgiveness and good things to happen. The Unity of Judgment and Mercy is Mercy – even the bad things are good in Hashem's grand design which we may not understand. The Shema *that sprung from Yaakov's heart expressed his epiphany – that his life of hardship and pain contributed to the magnificence of the* shelemut *of this moment, the reunion with his son Yosef.*

---

trait of thanksgiving is drawn from the traits of his father and grandfather, for thanksgiving is both love and self-sacrifice.

7. Netiv Ha'avoda 13, 1:120a: When a person serves Hashem out of love, he cleaves to Him as it is written [Deut. 11:22], "to love Hashem, your God, and to cleave to Him." Also see Netiv Ahavat Hashem 1, 2:39a.
8. Tiferet Yisrael 10:35b: If a person has fear of heaven, he cleaves to Him completely.

Vayechi

THE PRESENCE AT THE HEAD OF THE BED

47:31. And [Yaakov] said, "Swear to me," and [Yosef] swore to him, and Israel bowed at the head of the bed.

Rashi: He turned himself around toward the Divine Presence. From here the rabbis conclude that the Divine Presence is above the head of a sick person.

Gur Arye: Yaakov's illness is mentioned in the next verse [47:32], sometime after his meeting with Yosef. Rather than illness, the midrash is referring to a weakening of power which occasioned the presence of the *Shechina* above Yaakov's head. Worrying about his death and burial weakened him, and Hashem will "dwell with the crushed and lowly of spirit" [Isa. 57:15].[1]

Although Yosef had not yet carried out his promise, Yaakov

---

1. Netiv Hatorah 12, 1:52a: Hashem is close to the widow and the orphan, and He Himself fights their battles, as it is said, "I will dwell with the lowly of spirit." Netzach Yisrael 10:64a: There are two reasons the *Shechina* is with the sick. One, whenever something needs protection, His influence increases. Hashem places a natural survival force in a person, but when he falls ill, his nature changes, and he comes to need Hashem's protection. Secondly, He "dwells with the lowly of spirit," a special quality of Hashem to be with those who need Him. Chidushei Agadot on Ned. 40a, 2:19a: Since nature is faulty in a sick person, his survival depends on Hashem, for sickness is a departure from

bowed, indicating he was not at all concerned that the promised would not be kept.

MDK: Gur Arye is concerned that Rashi mentions Yaakov's illness before it occurs in the text. His answer is that, even before his illness, he was in a weakened state that required the closeness of the Shechina.

---

physical nature and Hashem transcends physical nature, and stations Himself above the head, where the transcendent spirituality of a person resides.

HOW RACHEL SAVED THE JEWISH PEOPLE TWICE

48:7. But as for me, when I came from Padan,
Rachel died on me in the land of Kenaan,...and
I buried her there on the road to Efrat.

Rashi: And I did not even bring her to Bet Lechem into the land [town] and I know you have feelings in your heart against me. But you should know I buried her there by Hashem's decree, so that she should be of aid to her children when Nevuzaradan would exile them. When they would pass there, Rachel would go out on to her grave and weep and seek mercy for them, as it says [Jer. 35:15–16]: "A voice is heard in the heights, Rachel crying for her children...," and Hashem answers her, "There is a reward for your act, and the children will return to their borders."

Gur Arye: Why did Rachel cry more than the other matriarchs? The answer is found in Midrash Eicha Rabbati [Pesikta 24]: Rachel speaks to the Holy One, blessed be He: What did my children do that You brought such punishment upon them? If it is idolatry and You are jealous of a "co-wife,"[2] did I not love my husband Yaakov, and did he not work seven years to marry me [29:20], and in the end my father gave him my sister to marry [29:26]. What did I do? I gave over our prearranged secret signs to my sister. I am flesh and blood, and You are the Merciful King, all the more reason to be merciful to them. Hashem answers, "There is a reward for your act, and your children will return from the land of the enemy."

Rachel understood that it was proper for Yaakov to have two wives. This world, as opposed to the World to Come, is a world

---

2. Ramban, Ex. 20:3: Since Israel is Hashem's precious one, He is jealous like a husband when she goes with another. Chidushei Agadot on Sanh. 103b, 3:240b: Idolatry is nothing, meaningless, for how could this dog be mentioned in the same breath as the Cause of Causes [*ila hailot*]? But from the standpoint of man, the idolater is marrying a co-wife alongside Hashem.

of division and separation,[3] and to confront this world, Yaakov's seed had to be diverse. Israel needed to be divided into two kingdoms, Yehuda and Efraim, only to join together in the days of Mashiach, and this could not happen if all of Yaakov's twelve sons came from one wife. The diversity of Israel would help it survive a tumultous history on its Land and a long, dangerous exile. Rachel saw this and loved him all the more, and accepted her sister as a co-wife. That same reasoning made it appropriate that Hashem be merciful to Israel, for the very existence of idolatry in this world is a consequence of a lack of unity in this world. "Hashem is our God, Hashem is One" is explained by Rashi [Deut. 6:4] to mean Hashem, who is our God now in this world, and not recognized as Hashem by the nations, will become the one God for all the nations in the World to Come, as it says [Zeph. 3:9], "Then I will switch the nations to a clear language, for all of them to call in the name of Hashem," and [Zech. 14:9], "on that day, Hashem will be One and His name One." This is all discussed in Netzach Yisrael [34].

The Congregation of Israel is named after Rachel[4] because she is the *akeret habayit* [essence of the home][5] and the others were secondary to her.[6] She was the reason Yaakov married Lavan's daughters. On her account the nation of Israel will return to its borders and connect with Hashem. She has the power to reverse the separation of her children from Hashem and their dispersion throughout the lands. She should not be buried in the Cave of the Patriarchs but, rather, out there on the road with her children. She was indeed rewarded for her act – she saved her

---

3. See 2:10[12]{59}, 23:2[4], and Netzach Yisrael 33, 152a-153b.
4. See Amos 5:15 and Jer. 31:19.
5. 29:31: And Rachel was *akara* [barren, principal]. BR 71:2: She was the essence of the house.
6. 31:4 and Ruth 4:11.

children, the Jewish People, from God's wrath, and assured the ultimate redemption.[7]

MDK: Rachel first saved the Children of Israel by giving over the secret signs to her sister Lea, which assured the diversity and discord evident throughout Jewish history, not to mention today. This diversity resulted in the honing of survival skills required for the exile. The selflessness of that act, allowing a rival wife in her home, influenced Hashem's decision to eventually end the exile.

---

7. Netzach Yisrael 1:11a: The woman is called "house" as Rabbi Yosi said [Git. 52a]: "I never called my wife 'my wife,' I only called my wife 'my house,' for Rachel was the *akeret habayit* of Yaakov, and house includes and unites everything in it. Therefore, Yaakov said that Rachel was buried on the road, closer to her people. There she has the potential to gather and unite her children now dispersed in exile.

SWORD AND BOW

48:22. And I have given you an extra portion [*shechem achat*] more than your brothers, which I took from the hand of the Emorites with my sword and my bow.

Rashi: When Shimon and Levi killed the men of Shechem, the surrounding tribes came to their defense, and Yaakov donned his battle gear to oppose them. Another interpretation: "My sword and my bow" refers to wisdom and prayer.

Gur Arye: Wisdom is called "sword" because it is sharp like a sword,[8] and prayer is referred to as "bow," because the tongue on which the prayers depend is often called "arrow,"[9] and the prayers of the righteous ascend skyward, slicing through the upper and lower spheres. Mind, thought, and intent are the bow that launches the arrow of tongue and prayer. However Onkelos, following the *Gemara* [B.B. 123a], translates the phrase, "my prayer and my request," suggesting sword is prayer[10] and bow is request. *Keshet* [bow] connotes *koshi* [toughness, difficulty], for it is a more difficult, focused form of prayer. *Tefila* [prayer] appeals to Hashem's mercy, so that He reconsider the result of strict judgment in light of the person's merit. *Techina* [request] appeals to gratuitous kindness [*chesed*], which is undeserved [*chinam*], and requires a more dynamic force, like the arrow.

---

8. See Hag. 15b and Onkelos 3:24.
9. See Jer. 9:7 and Ar. 16b. Netiv Halashon 1, 2:64b: The tongue is not a physical thing, for physical things move at a slower pace. The action of the tongue is fast like an arrow and kills like an arrow. Netiv Hatzeniut 4, 2:110b: The tongue has the form of an arrow. Rashi 49:23: The archers are so called because their tongues are like arrows.
10. Deut. R. 1:10: Moshe's prayer is like a sword that slices and cuts in an unstoppable fashion. Se Chidushei Agadot on B.B. 123b, 3:125a.

MDK: Maharal exploits conflicting interpretations of "sword" and "bow" to explore the meaning and mechanism of different types of prayer.

WHERE IS YEHUDA'S ROD TODAY?

49:10. The rod shall not depart from Yehuda nor a lawgiver from between his feet, until Shilo arrives, and his will be an assemblage of nations.

Rashi: The rod, that is, the rulership, shall not depart from Yehuda from King David onward. This refers to the exilarchs in Bavel who ruled with the rod, for they were appointed by royal authority. "Lawgiver" refers to the princes, teachers of the students [from Hillel onward]. Shilo refers to the King Mashiach, for the kingship is his [shelo], as Onkelos renders. The aggadic midrash [Yalkut Shimoni 160] explains Shilo as a contraction of shai lo, a gift to him, as it says [Ps. 76:12], "They will deliver a gift [shai] to the revered one."

Gur Arye: Rashi means Yehuda, that is the Kingdom of the House of David, shall rule from the ascension of David onward up to and including the days of King Mashiach. Ramban, in his disputation with the apostate Jew and Catholic priest, Don Pablo Christiani, in Barcelona in 1273 [Kitvei Haramban 1, 304:11 and 13] is asked, if this account of Yaakov's blessing is true, how do the Jews account for the absence of Yehuda's rule now? The princes do not rule any longer in the Land of Israel, nor do the exilarchs in Bavel![11] The answer lies in a careful reading of the text – it does not say, "the rod will not pass from Israel." Israel, on account of its sins, is not fit to have its king, but when their true ruler returns, he will be from Yehuda, for the rod will never pass from Yehuda. The Kingdom of the House of David is waiting, rod in hand, for the coming of Shilo and the ultimate redemption.

A complementary approach to account for the validity of Yaakov's blessing of Yehuda in our time takes note of the irreversibility

---

11. Sanh. 38a: The son of David will not come until the two dynasties will terminate – the exilarchs in Bavel and the princes in the Land of Israel.

of the verb *yasir* [permanently depart]. The Kingdom of the House of David is called "fallen" because it stands ready to be rebuilt.[12] The pieces lie there in a heap, not like a mansion that requires construction from the foundation up, but like a booth [*succa*] that can simply be erected from the pieces in the heap. In the words of the prophet [Amos 9:11], "On that day I will erect the fallen *succa* of David." The King Mashiach waits, holding the rod that never was removed from Yehuda. May the Merciful One erect for us the fallen *succa* of David, speedily in our time.

MDK: On its face, history would seem to conflict with Rashi's assertion that Yehuda would always rule. Gur Arye answers with Ramban's disputation, that the verse means that when Israel deserves a king, i.e., Mashiach, he will come from Yehuda. The scepter has never left the House of David.

---

12. Netzach Yisrael 35:158b.

OUR FATHER YAAKOV LIVES

> 49:33. When Yaakov finished instructing his sons, he drew his feet onto the bed: he expired [*vayigva*] and was brought in to his people.

Rashi: But dying [mita] is not said of him. From here our rabbis said [Ta'an. 5a] that our father Yaakov did not die.

Gur Arye: There is a remarkable hidden matter in this about which I will give you a hint – perhaps you will understand. It is known that death is a termination and a *katze* [outer boundary, end]. If something has no outer boundary, it has no death. Consider three dots on a line – the middle dot has no access to the end of the line. Yaakov is that middle dot, bounded by Avraham his grandfather on one side and Yitzchak his father on the other.[13] He is the one who reconciles the other two.[14] That is why Yaakov is called "Yeshurun" [Isa. 44:2], meaning *yashar* [upright, honest, true].[15] The end happens when something or someone departs from *yosher*. Bilam said, "Let my soul die the death of *yesharim* and let my afterlife be like theirs" [Num. 23:10], meaning because of their uprightness, their death is not death in the sense of their entitlement to a portion of the World to Come.[16]

Why is it that only Yaakov, and not the other patriarchs, is said to live eternally? Avraham's main trait was *chesed*, kindness, and he called the Holy Place, "mountain," as it is written, "on the Mountain of Hashem He will be seen" [22:12]. Kindness

---

13. 28:11[17]: Yaakov is the root and the connection and the unification of the patriarchs – the middle stave. See Tiferet Yisrael 50:156a.
14. Sifra, introduction: Rabbi Yishmael said…if there are two verses that contradict each other, a third verse can come and reconcile between them.
15. Or Chadash 220a: Something *yashar* has no end – that is why Yaakov does not die. Also see Chidushei Agadot on Shab. 118a, 1:54b.
16. Derasha al Hatorah 24b.

without Judgment may allow an attachment to Hashem under extraordinary circumstances, such as the unique personage of an Avraham, or at Hashem's Place. A nation cannot be built solely on the trait of kindness. Yitzchak's trait was *din*, Judgment, and he called the Holy Place, "field," as it is written, "and Yitzchak went out to pray in the field" [24:63]. A nation cannot be built on unmitigated Judgment. Yaakov's trait was *rachamim* [mercy, love] and he referred to the Holy Place as *bayit*, house, as it is written, and Yaakov called the place of El, "the House of El" [*Bet El*].

The Holy Temple is the place where Hashem has a connection to, and an attachment with, the lower spheres. Avraham's kindness is like a mountain, for kindness has greatness just as a mountain has greatness. If a person is fair to others, he deals honestly and with exact propriety, he may fail to go out of his way for others, to go beyond the letter of the law. The kind person is not so exact and does more than what is required of him – this is his greatness, as it is written, "Your righteousness is like the Mountains of God" [Ps. 36:6]. This is the attachment Avraham has with Hashem, and he calls His Place "mountain."

Yitzchak, who endured near-death on the Altar, was constantly aware of Hashem's Power over him, and his awe and fear of Hashem, the God of Judgment, characterized the nature of his attachment to Hashem. He conducted himself with correctness and exactitude, which is also a Godly trait. He called the Holy Place, "field," for a field is flat and straight, just like Judgment.

Yaakov's trait is Mercy, which is a synthesis of Kindness and Judgment. Mercy is the essential and permanent connection, corresponding to his name for the Holy Place – "house." The mountain and the field are places of temporary connection to Hashem, but the House of Holiness, the *Bet Hamikdash*, the Holy Temple, is the permanent abode of the Divine Presence. *Rachamim*, Mercy, means love and connectedness. Targum Onkelos renders *oheiv*, love, as *merachamohi*, which means mercy [25:28]. Love is essential connectedness and attachment, as we see when a parent loves a child, that parent has mercy on that child.[17]

Only Yaakov, of all the beloved patriarchs, is eternal, just as the nation he founds is eternal,[18] for his loving attachment to Hashem is eternal. This everlasting life is spoken of in the Torah: "And you, who cleave to Hashem your God, are all alive today" [Deut. 4:4]. Why, then, can we not all achieve the status of "not dying"? Because the physical-material nature of our bodies precludes this, even if we would be able to attach ourselves to Him through *rachamim*. Yaakov, having "expired," was a soul no longer attached to his physicality. Now his *rachamim* confers immortality. *Am Yisrael chai – od avinu chai.* The nation of Israel lives – our father still lives.

MDK: Strictly speaking, Maharal does not answer the question of why it is only Yaakov who did not die. Certainly others fulfill the criteria mentioned. But he clearly answers it in an allegorical/lyrical/spiritual sense, which brings us to a better understanding of the character of the patriarchs, a fitting closure to Gur Arye's treatment of the Book of Genesis.

---

17. Netzach Yisrael 52:197a.
18. Avot Derabbi Natan 34:10: Ten are called "alive" – Hashem, Torah, Israel, saint, Garden of Eden, Land of Israel, charity, light, water, and World to Come.

Abbreviations

BOOKS OF THE BIBLE

Amos	Amos.	Judg.	Judges.
Chron. I	Chronicles I.	Kings I	Kings I.
Chron. II	Chronicles II.	Kings II	Kings II.
Dan.	Daniel.	Lam.	Lamentations.
Deut.	Deuteronomy.	Lev.	Leviticus.
Eccl.	Ecclesiastes.	Mal.	Malachi.
Est.	Esther.	Mic.	Micah.
Ex.	Exodus.	Nah.	Nahum.
Ezek.	Ezekiel.	Neh.	Nehemiah.
Ezra	Ezra.	Num.	Numbers.
Gen.	Genesis.	Ob.	Obadiah.
Hab.	Habakkuk.	Prov.	Proverbs.
Hag.	Haggai.	Ps.	Psalms.
Hos.	Hosea.	Ruth	Ruth.
Isa.	Isaiah.	Sam. I	Samuel I.
Jer.	Jeremiah.	Sam. II	Samuel II.
Job	Job.	S.O.S.	Song of Songs.
Joel	Joel.	Zech.	Zechariah.
Jonah	Jonah.	Zep.	Zephaniah.
Josh.	Joshua.		

TRACTATES OF THE TALMUD

Ab.	Aboth.
'Ar.	'Arakin.
'A.Z.	'Abodah Zarah.
B.B.	Baba Bathra.
Bek.	Bekoroth.
Ber.	Berakoth.
Bez.	Bezah.
Bik.	Bikkurim.
B.K.	Baba Kamma.
B.M.	Baba Mezi'a.
'Er., 'Erub.	'Erubin.
Git.	Gittin.
Hag.	Hagigah.
Hul.	Hullin.
Mak.	Makkoth.
Meg.	Megillah.
Men.	Menahoth.
Mik.	Mikwa'oth.
M.K.	Mo'ed Katan.
Naz.	Nazir.
Ned., Neda.	Nedarim.
Neg.	Nega'im.
Nid.	Niddah.
Pes.	Pesahim.
R.H.	Rosh Hashanah.
Sanh.	Sanhedrin.
Shab.	Shabbath.
Sheb.	Shebi'ith.
Sot.	Sotah.
Suk.	Sukkah.
Ta' or Ta'an.	Ta'anith.
Yeb.	Yebamoth.
Yom.	Yoma.
Zeb.	Zebahim.